MW01598401

A
SMALL COLLECTION
OF
SPECIALIZED
SPREADS

VOLUME THREE

A
SMALL COLLECTION
OF
SPECIALIZED
SPREADS

**BY A GROUP OF FINE CARD READERS
FROM AROUND THE WORLD**

Vol. Three

Edited by Coleman Stevenson

The Dark Exact, LLC / Portland, OR

© 2022 The Dark Exact, LLC

PO Box 11865
Portland, OR 97211
www.etsy.com/shop/TheDarkExact
www.instagram.com/darkexact

Book design, graphics, and illustrations

by Coleman Stevenson

ISBN 978-0-9992520-9-3

This book is dedicated to

CONTENTS

INTRODUCTION TO VOLUME THREE

A NOTE FROM THE EDITOR

In the introductions to Volumes One and Two of this book series I have offered my advice for crafting spreads, discussed my experiences using them in readings, and answered a variety of collected questions from students and other practitioners about "best" practices. If you're interested in that specific content, I invite you to reference the previous volumes. In this volume, I'm not going to talk directly about using and making spreads. Instead, I'm opening a path to those topics in more unconventional ways with the help of some very talented friends.

This introductory section includes a liberating exploration of "divinatory poetics" by writer and card reader Selah Saterstrom. Her "Notes on Card Spreads" will encourage you to deeply consider what it is we do when we consult our oracles ("Where does divination happen? It happens in us. It happens between us.") and how we might want to engage differently with these processes.

Saterstrom's beautiful piece is followed by two experimental spread-generating spreads/exercises, one by Lars Sparby, a regular contributor to this book series, and one made collaboratively by Erik Arneson and me for our classes on spread design. They are strange and wonderful to work through, and the process of using them will teach you a lot about the logic of spread creation.

Like the other volumes, the spreads in this book are a combination of my own creations and the work of many other excellent readers. My contributions include a few individual spreads and reading processes, as well as the group of seasonal spreads I crafted for the equinoxes and solstices (or for use at other times of transition). One of those appeared in a previous volume, but I like the easy reference of having all four in one place now that the set is complete.

The other spreads in this book cover the usual wide range of themes. Lengths and level of complexity are intentionally varied. As always, you'll find simple, straightforward, practical spreads, but you'll also find meandering experiments in divination, some bordering on the surreal. I'm particularly THRILLED to announce that this volume has works from students in the Spread Design Basics class that Erik and I offered last winter. I was so impressed with everyone's creative and original work and am honored to be able to include some of those insightful spreads here for you all to use.

Now, let the exploration begin...

NOTES ON CARD SPREADS

A Small & Partial Excerpt from the Essay "Divinatory Poetics"

Selah Saterstrom

1. Divination provides an opportunity to risk having a different sort of relationship with uncertainty.

2. Divination is a place where we might engage with the invisible. The invisible might appear as "nothing" and nothing is also a *plurality of intensities.*

3. Divination is a place...
Where? Where does divination happen?

It happens in us. It happens between us. And also, it happens elsewhere. Like the energy of healing, it does not depend on linear time to present. It is multivalent.

A spread of cards is always simultaneous, a mouth with a thousand tongues, but as the divinatory moves through the devoted reader (and out the reader's mouth) it finds a way to calibrate to the frequency of human ears.

When I go into the divinatory realms, I will sometimes say, as a way to begin the reading: *As I enter the Field—or—As I lean into the Flux...* as if I'm entering a space. Indeed: there are *sensations.* In this space/realm there are, it seems to me, innumerable frequencies. Furthermore, this field allows contradiction and paradox without needing to resolve either.

At times, the client's questions are a sort of anchor that might help a reader attune to particular patterns within this extraordinary, humming field, this sanctuary of flux. A card spread is a piece of lace cast onto the inky top-coat of the fertile void. It is a spider web that you walk through, face first, during the long night. It's the pattern cast by decay-traces inside the abandoned _____ (chapel, bouchère, swimming pool, locket, and so on).

Sometimes though, once inside the divinatory field, one can loiter. In such cases, one might hear the ancestors and helpers gossiping (they know before we know). One can hear other sounds, too.

There is a sound in the Flux right now that I am unable to place. It bothers me.

4.

Camille Roy:
Narrative provides context so that the rupturing of identity is recognizable.

Divination is a place where we might see where or how we are out of alignment. It maintains the potential to put people in touch with observations, strategies, and paradigms so that they might come back into alignment. Less concerned about fixed outcomes, divination soaks its roots in liberation.

5. The best hermeneutic posture one can bring to the oracular event is almost always loving curiosity.

6. Sometimes divination is done with cards. A popular method.

One way to think about cards is to imagine each card as an archetype which opens into an archive. Within, there are vast and shimmering networks, underwritten by interstitial catacombs. And the reader's body is also an archive, a living one, so that when these two archival sites touch, capacity increases; the needle skips across the surface of the record. Sort of like a mirror that becomes, for a moment, unfixed.

Like language, that unstable medium of lamentation and celebration, a card's meaning cannot be exhausted. It will never be fixed. It will never, alas, arrive.

What is the quality of energy that zips across the nervous system of a card? Alchemy.

What do you call a spread of cards? A sheet of lace, a spider web, a pile of rotting roses on the charnel grounds, a screen door, slapping the frame. A formation of stars to be born under. A handle to dovetail into/with the divinatory field so that it can be brought to one's lips, for a long, cool drink.

A way, I wouldn't say to *organize* the energy, but rather to *see(r)* the energy in its *bloom* iteration.

7.

Blanchot:
Let us count, rather, on disarray.

This is a fine sentiment to suggest what a card spread might embrace. By "disarray" I don't mean an absence of arrangement or disposition. I mean to queer the cogent, the linear, the binary. There is nothing straight about divination.

Divination is located in a field beyond the organizing categories of our most-oft cited tenses: past/present/future. Cards, and in their formations (spread patterns), are touchstones that lead us to an interior, somatic vocabulary. That we might speak. That we might invite in the story that helps the client, the community member, the loved one, the self.

A popular prayer I learned from ghosts + women in my family—

The Diviner's Prayer

Lord, may me and mine be on the fortuitous side of the interruption.

UNCANNY SPREAD-BUILDING SPREAD

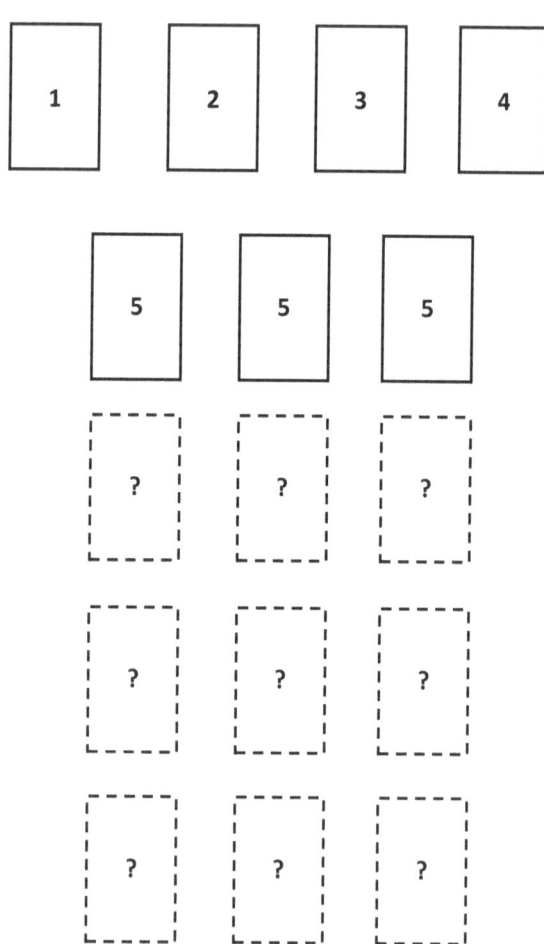

For an example of a spread created with this exercise, refer to p. 82.

UNCANNY SPREAD-BUILDING SPREAD

Erik Arneson & Coleman Stevenson

This is a spread for designing spreads! Follow these instructions:

1. Understanding the Context
This card tells you the entire purpose or theme of the spread. Here are some examples:
- A Pentacles card could indicate a business-related spread.
- Cups could indicate a spread about relationships.
- Swords could be a spread about communication or learning.
- Wands could be about inspiration, goals, or creativity.
- A Major Arcana card could indicate matters of personal growth, life purpose, or another truly life-changing context for the spread!

2. Providing Direction
Is this spread going to be more about insight or action? This card can help you figure that out. For example, a Cups card in this position could indicate that the spread is about action, particularly interactions with other people. Meanwhile, an introspective card like the Moon or High Priestess could indicate that your spread will be more about turning inward and providing insight.

3. Counting the Parameters
Use the number on the card to determine the size of your spread. For example, if you draw the 6 of Cups, you would design a 6-card spread. (To give yourself enough to work with, but keep the spread manageable, if you draw a card with a number lower than 3, create a 3-card spread; if you draw a card with a number over 12, create a 12-card spread.

4. Determining Shape

A "fun" placement: let this card help you pick the shape for your spread! For example (referencing Rider Waite Smith imagery), if you draw the 10 of Cups, you might let the rainbow of chalices inspire you to shape your spread like an arch. The Tower could lead you to design your spread in the shape of a lightning bolt. The 9 of Pentacles could inspire a spiral reading like a snail's shell, or the 8 of Cups the outline of a person with a walking stick.

5. Positions

Now that you have the general context, size, and shape of your new spread, it's time to use more cards to determine what each position in the spread indicates. You already determined the size and shape of the spread with Cards 3 & 4, so draw that many cards face down, and arrange them accordingly. Flip the cards over one at a time and interpret each to create a question or topic that its position will indicate in that spread. For example:

- If you are designing a business spread and draw the Ace of Cups for a position card, that position might be about a helpful workplace relationship.
- If you draw a "travelling" card like the 6 of Swords or the Chariot for the business-related spread you're building, that position might indicate something about business travel or advancement in a job.

Refining Your Spread

Once you have determined the meanings of the positions, you can refine the spread. You might need to move cards around, alter the shape of the spread, draw more position cards or even remove some cards. Though it is entirely possible that this method will uncannily create a perfect cartomancy spread on its own, you should not be afraid to play with the results so that it works for you and your querents.

THE RANDOM ESOTERIC SPREAD THINGAMAJIG

Or How to Generate Your Own Completely Unique Tarot Spread in Just Six Simple Steps*

Lars Sparby

As modern-day cartomancers, we tend to forget about Tarot's original connection with playing cards and games in general. Here I have attempted to bring the two just a little bit closer together again. By using the following post-modern method, I invite you to adopt a playful mindset and to simply have some fun with the way you approach Tarot. **To make the most of this spread you will need a standard six-sided die or any other suitable mechanism for generating random numbers from one to six.**

* For an example of a spread created using this exercise, refer to p. 76.

STEP ONE: Name Your Spread
Roll six times, once for each table, A-F. (Optional: If you don't care about your spread having a unique name, or if you are in a rush, you may skip this preliminary step. Alternatively, you can go back and roll on these tables after the rest of the spread has been rolled up.)

A
1. The
2. A/An
3. Ye
4. My (or "your name" e.g. "Lars Sparby's")
5. Some
6. That

B
1. Telestic
2. Perplexing
3. Numinous
4. Mystifying
5. Anagogic
6. Uncanny

C	D
1. Oracle	1. Of
2. Machine	2. Concerning
3. Mirror	3. Beyond
4. Window	4. Dealing with
5. Kaleidoscope	5. About
6. Speculum	6. Regarding

E	F
1. Forbidden	1. Scrutiny
2. Amazing	2. Probing
3. Extraordinary	3. Foreshadowing
4. Startling	4. Omens
5. Astounding	5. Revelation
6. Visionary	6. Prognostication

STEP TWO: Determine the Number of Cards in the Spread
Roll just once on the table below.

1. Three cards
2. Four cards
3. Five cards
4. Six cards
5. Seven cards

STEP THREE: Working Out the Layout
Roll once, or choose one.

1. Line
2. Geometric shape (Triangle, Square, Pentagram/Pentagon, Hexagram/Hexagon, Septagram/ Septagon, Octagram/Optagon)
3. Tableaux
4. Outsource. Borrow a shape/layout from another unrelated spread, either from this book itself, another book in this series, or from somewhere else entirely.

5. Figurative. Mimic an object, human/animal anatomy, or some sort of natural/supernatural phenomenon.
6. Random pattern. Throw several dice (or any small objects you have around) equal to the number of cards onto a piece of paper and mark the positions where they fall.

STEP FOUR: Resolve the Meaning of the Card Positions
Roll once for each card in the spread to determine the category, then roll once more on that category's corresponding table to assign the card's specific meaning. It is possible to get duplicate positions, and in that case, you may or may not want to re-roll, depending on the level of surrealism you are after.

1. What   2. When   3. Where   4. Who   5. How   6. Why

WHAT
1. What you are secretly scared of
2. What is threatening you
3. What you must do before it's too late
4. What aspect of yourself you have been neglecting
5. What makes you special
6. What source of energy you can tap into

WHEN
1. When you should start
2. When you should stop
3. When you should compromise
4. When you can make a move
5. When you will change
6. When the time is right

WHERE

1. Where you can find inspiration
2. Where you need to focus
3. Where to look again
4. Where to investigate further
5. Where you must go deeper
6. Where there's a hidden treasure to be found

WHO

1. Who can teach you a lesson
2. Whom you can trust to help in this matter
3. Who can say what you need to hear
4. Who you really are in this scenario
5. Whom you can count on for support
6. Who you can become

HOW

1. How to diffuse the situation
2. How it will end
3. How you can strike a balance
4. How you can get to the truth of the matter
5. How it's possible to improve the conditions
6. How to approach

WHY

1. Why you feel the way you do
2. Why you must do the right thing
3. Why you should care
4. Why this happened to you
5. Why you shouldn't care
6. Why it is so difficult

STEP FIVE: The Read

After the spread has been generated, it's time to read with it. Make sure you have sketched out a layout and that you have written down all the positional meanings before you shuffle your deck. Proceed with your standard method for pulling cards.

STEP SIX: Conclusion and/or Adding a Twist to It All (Optional)

Once all the cards have been laid down and you've done a preliminary overview of your interpretation, if you want, you can roll on this table to add another effect.

1. A flashback to a past event! Draw one more card.
2. A new piece of evidence that may change everything. Draw one more card.
3. An unforeseen turn of events that will complicate matters further. Draw one more card.
4. One of the previous cards turns out to be a red herring and contains false information. Determine which card it is by rolling.
5. Cliffhanger! The read ends here. No additional card is to be pulled. To be continued next read.
6. Reversal! It turns out that the cards have been revealed in reversed chronological order. Please move the cards into their new correct positions (e.g. card six to position one and card one to position six, card five becomes card two, and card two is now five, etc.)

Designer notes: The main inspiration for this spread is all manner of random charts and tables found in various pen and paper roleplaying games, tabletop miniature games, and board games. As such, I initially wanted to include more complicated tables that utilized different sorts of polyhedral dice as well as dice mechanics that would result in a more bell-like distribution. However, for the sake of simplicity, I chose to go with a single six-sided die. Feel free to expand the tables provided above. I particularly recommend adding your own entries to the tables.

SEASONAL SPREADS INSPIRED BY THE EQUINOXES & SOLSTICES

by Coleman Stevenson

SPRING EQUINOX SPREAD

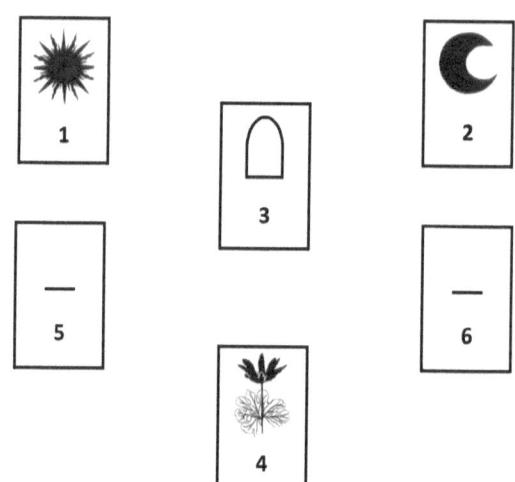

SPRING EQUINOX SPREAD

Coleman Stevenson

This spread can be used not just at the Spring Equinox but any time greater balance is needed.

1. **Day:** Conscious need or desire.

2. **Night:** Subconscious need or desire.

3. **The Archway:** A moment of equilibrium that opens a gateway to something new. (This could be the way to balance the first two cards. It might also indicate a new opportunity.)

4. **New Growth:** What can return to you, rejuvenated, once balance is restored.

5/6 — **Additional cards** may be placed to the left and right of the archway if desired. These positions could be reserved for specific questions or used as clarifying cards for information revealed in the rest of the reading.

* Instead of pulling one card for #4, you could expand this position for a more detailed sense of what's emerging for you. I like to reference the symbolism of the plants emerging around me at this time and use those meanings to contextualize up to three additional cards for this position of New Growth.

SUMMER SOLSTICE SPREAD

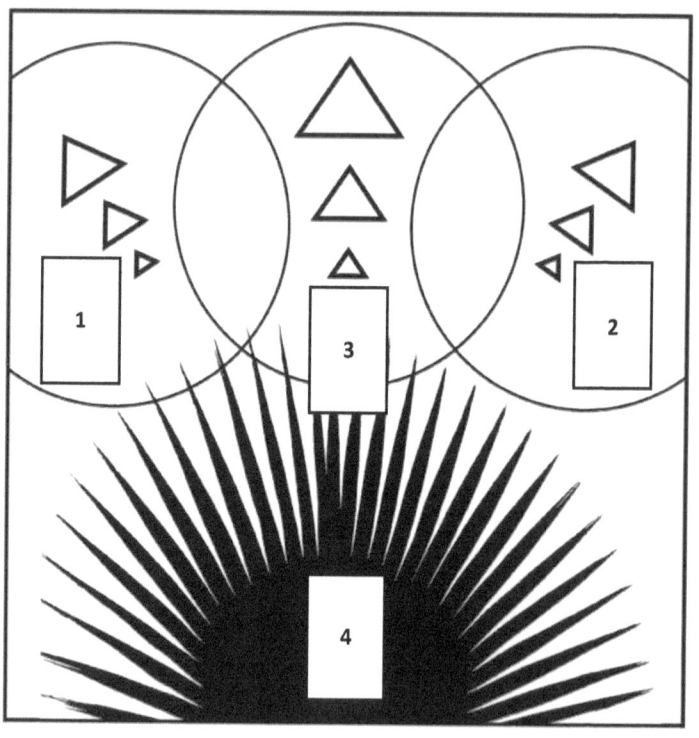

SUMMER SOLSTICE SPREAD

Coleman Stevenson

This spread can be used not just at the Summer Solstice but any time greater self-confidence is needed.

For the first three positions, draw <u>up to three cards</u> each. For the final position, draw <u>one card</u>.

1. **Left Circle:** How your efforts are showing results.

2. **Right Circle:** How to continue that growth.

3. **Center Circle:** The light within; source of confidence.

4. **Bottom:** The external light that provides warmth and motivates you to continue.

AUTUMN EQUINOX SPREAD

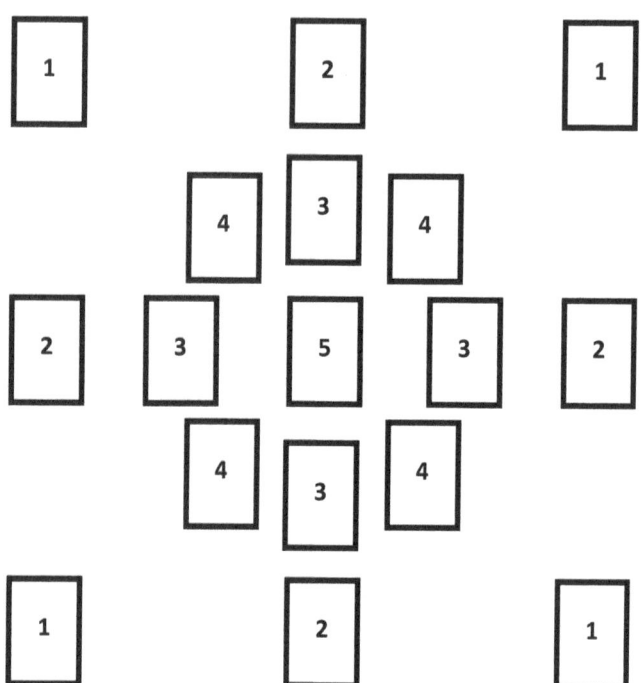

AUTUMN EQUINOX SPREAD

Coleman Stevenson

This spread can be used not only around the Autumn Equinox but at any transitional time. For positions 1-4, draw up to four cards each. For position 5, draw one card.

1. **What bloomed for you last season:** These cards indicate successes and/or lessons learned.

2. **What is going to seed now:** These cards reveal things that are winding down, in need of rest, or no longer needed in your life.

3. **What to store up for winter:** These cards suggest resources you may need in the coming months.

4. **Seeds to sew for spring:** These cards indicate ideas requiring further consideration before action is taken.

5. **A personal symbol to work with this season:** This is a tangible object to serve as a talisman / point of reflection, determined by the imagery on the card or something the card description calls to mind.

WINTER SOLSTICE SPREAD

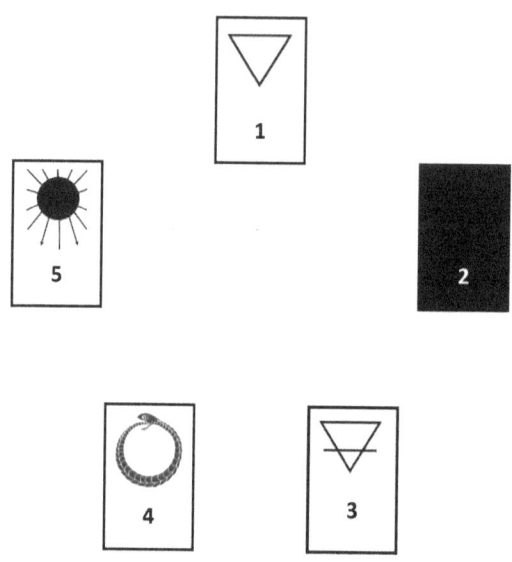

This spread first appeared in Volume Two, but I'm reprinting it in this book so that all four seasons are together.

WINTER SOLSTICE SPREAD

Coleman Stevenson

This spread can be used not just at the Winter Solstice but at any time to encourage rebirth / a new cycle when cleansing is needed.

1. **What has been washed away in the previous season:** Something that's finished, cleansed from your life/psyche, something you no longer need.

2. **A message from the Darkness of the Longest Night:** Something you need to know in order to move forward.

3. **What to bury:** Like a bulb that will flower in spring, something to prepare for, work on; a new possibility to consider.

4. **How to support root growth:** What you need in order to feel rejuvenated/rested for the next season.

5. **Rebirth of the Sun:** What will be revealed as the light returns.

A COLLECTION OF SPREADS

**and other approaches to the cards
by a variety of creative readers**

AT HOME: A DAY-LONG SPREAD/ "EGG HUNT"

Coleman Stevenson

For years now, I've worked from home, a practice that many more people have become familiar with in recent years for reasons of safety in a global pandemic. There are some weeks that my contact with the external world is very limited for days at a time. While this is part of my process, and helps me be more productive as an artist, it removes the series of small interactions with other people and the outside environment that would have organically occurred had I been out and about, moving through the course of a day. Sometimes it is those minor moments that provide more color and little shocks of insight into our lives. This "spread" is a way to put back some of those "encounters" into a day spent alone at home.

OPTION #1: Self-Generated

1. This step is best done the night before, just before going to sleep but could also be done first thing in the morning. Shuffle and cut your deck as you would for any reading.

2. Locate a place in each room of your home (or various spots around your room if you live in a studio or shared housing) that you habitually use/encounter every day. For example, places I know I will pay attention to every day are the bathroom sink, coffee maker, work table/desk, windowsill, dresser drawer, closet, and nightstand. Choose up to 10 locations. (You could even keep this very simple and place only one card-of-the-day in a single key location you know you'll encounter at a certain time.)

3. Drawing from the top of the deck, place one card (face down) in each of your selected locations. DO NOT look at the cards when you place them.

4. Go about your day as you normally would. Each time you encounter one of the cards, turn it over and interpret it. You might think about it as a person you've passed on the street or were next to on the bus (especially for Major Arcana and Court cards). What conversation does that card strike up with you? If the card has a lot of scenic imagery, imagine that you are traveling past, taking in this scene through the window of a vehicle or at the speed of some other mode of transportation. What catches your eye and your interest? Why?

OPTION #2: With a Partner

1. In this variation, have someone else place the cards for you in locations of their choosing. They can leave the cards (face down) in the open or find less obvious hiding places (inside cabinets and drawers, underneath objects you habitually use, etc.) The idea here, though, is that these locations would still be places you interact with daily, and the cards would still be chosen randomly by this assistant.

2. Follow the rest of the instructions as outlined in Option #1.

PALIMPSEST SPREAD

Coleman Stevenson

This spread was inspired by a visit to a friend's home during her extensive remodeling project. In a corner of the room where I slept, she had removed layers of paint and wallpaper to see what was underneath, revealing a rich history of choices made by the previous occupants of the house. For this reading, you will be examining a progression of time—days, weeks, months, years, decades—and the choices made at those times that have informed what came after. The number of cards will be determined by how far back you want to explore.

1. Shuffle the deck as you normally would. When you feel ready to select cards, cut the deck.

2. Take the bottom card and place it face down in front of you. Continue pulling cards from the deck, moving from the bottom up, placing them face down on top of the others already selected. The final card will be the top card in the deck. Pull one card for each increment of time within the chosen period. For example, an examination of the layers of the last five years living in a certain place would consist of five cards.

3. Read the cards as a series (bottom to top) to understand how you have arrived at your present place/state. Consider how the imagery of pairs of subsequent cards overlaps. Imagine that parts of the card underneath are peeking through the card above. What is revealed by this palimpsest?

4. After these layers have been unearthed and evaluated, reshuffle the remaining cards in the deck, cut, and turn over the top card to determine the new "wallpaper" you might select as you continue forward from this point.

SELF-LOVE & INTEGRATION

1 2 3

SELF-LOVE & INTEGRATION

Selah Saterstrom

The goal: to bring loving curiosity to any intel that emerges.

Position 1: Before turning over the card, name a wound—ancient or new—that you want to bring loving curiosity to.

This card, once revealed, will offer a narrative/clue/indicator of an event that this particular wound links into or passes through in your personal story.

Position 2: This card, once revealed, offers the gift of wisdom you earned through surviving that particular experience.

Position 3: This card, once revealed, offers information about how to integrate this wisdom into your present-day experience, that it might be a blessing to you.

FINDING THE THREAD

1 2 3

FINDING THE THREAD

Amanda Bell

All too often we find ourselves on the path, going full speed ahead, diving into whatever is in front of us, only to realize we've misplaced the thread that leads us to our goal, our purpose, our future self.

This spread is for finding that thread, reconnecting to our future self in tangible ways that help us navigate our way through. This spread also relies on your sense of sight. After you lay all three cards out let your eyes seek out the part of the image that pings you.

Card 1: Where you hold on. This is the part of the thread that your present self is connected to.

Card 2: This is the center of the thread. It is the through line between you and your future self. Find the story in this card, in this image, and center here. The connection cards on either side tell you the how-to.

Card 3: This is where your future self holds their part of the thread. This is the place that connects you to your future.

URÐARBRUNNR - THE COUNCIL OF THE NORNS

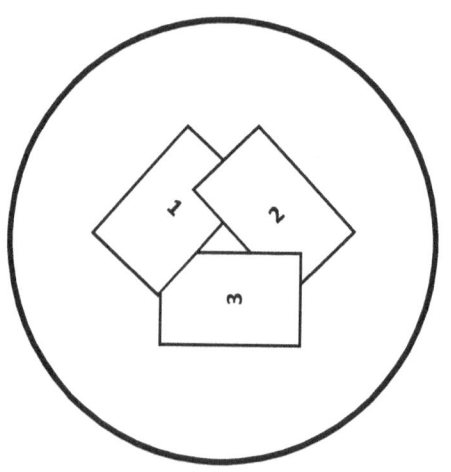

URÐARBRUNNR - THE COUNCIL OF THE NORNS

Lars Sparby

The goal is to foretell
From the seat of the sages
At Urd's well
I saw and I was silent
I saw and I reflected
Recovering mankind's mysteries
I heard the reasoning of the runes
Whose counsel was not restrained
At the High One's hollow
Inside Odin's hall
This is what I retained
- *Hávamál*[1]

In Norse mythology, beneath the world tree Yggdrasil, we are told there are three wells, Mímisbrunnr, Hvergelmir, and Urðarbrunnr. (Snorri Sturluson assigned one well for each of Yggdrasil's roots). Of these three, probably the most well-known is the latter, Urðarbrunnr, more commonly referred to as The Well of Urdr. This well is located in Asgard and is associated with a trio of complex deities called Nornir, which are named Urðr, Verðandi, and Skuld respectively. These three beings tend to Yggdrasil, keeping this tree of life alive and evergreen with their watering and care. They are also said to rule over people's destiny and their time of death. Because of this relation to destiny, they are very often linked to the ancient Greek Moirae, also called the three Fates. Although there are obvious similarities, the Moirae and Nornir are not the same. In fact, defining the Nornir with any authority is incredibly difficult.

As with most things relating to Old Norse history, clear distinctions are practically non-existent. Case in point, we get various descriptions of Nornir, and they are variously represented as Æsir, valkyries, fylgjar, dwarves, elves, jotnir, and dísir amongst other names, so it is safe to say that they remain immensely elusive. It is also important to mention that there are many more Nornir than just Urðr, Verðandi, and Skuld as referred to above. You can have a good Norn or a bad Norn, and it is even stated that each individual is assigned their own personal Norn when they are born, a concept remarkably comparable to a guardian angel or Daimon for instance. All this preamble is to provide some context as to why I am challenging the preconception of the Nornir exclusively corresponding to the temporal perception of the Past - Present - Future abstraction that has become the norm.

By reversing the order in which these Nornir are usually presented, and approaching them from an etymological and more authentic historic frame of reference, I am imparting the following adaptation that can be used as a divination[2] meditation:

1. Skuld: What I ought to become.

2. Verðandi: What I am becoming.

3. Urðr: What I have become.

Without taking up too much space and avoiding going into too many technical details, I will conclude with a brief explanation of the etymology of the three names:

Skuld derives from the Old Norse verb *skulu*, which means something that "needs to occur" or "should become." It also relates to "debt" and "guilt" in Norwegian as well as the word "should" in English.

Both *Urðr* and *Verðandi* come from the Old Norse word *verða*, meaning ""to become," and they are believed to represent different tenses. *Urðr* may mean "that which became" or "that which happened," and *Verðandi*, "that which is happening." Lastly, it is important to maintain that the words or names in and of themselves do not imply chronological periods in Old Norse.

---

[1] Please note that this is my own artistic rendition and transmutation of stanza 111 from the *Hávamál* poem.

[2] Despite this spread having been designed with runes in mind, it works equally well with other systems, like Tarot, Lenormand, or Oracle cards.

CREATIVE COLLABORATION SPREAD

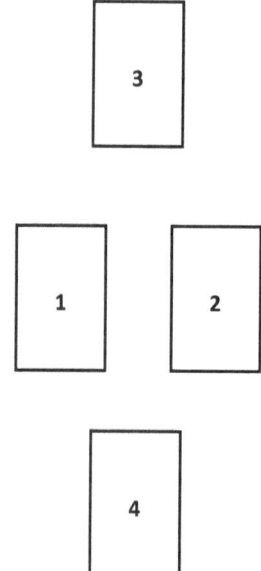

CREATIVE COLLABORATION SPREAD

Jess Rollar

A tool for artists and makers:

1. What needs to be noted and penciled in? (This is something to think about.)

2. What can be glued into place? (Look at this like the original goal of the project.)

3. This outside influence should be considered. (This can be advice to bring in, inspiration to tap into, etc.)

4. What can you personally add to this project? (Your strength or skill that can be brought to the collaborative table.)

THE FOUR METALLIC RULES

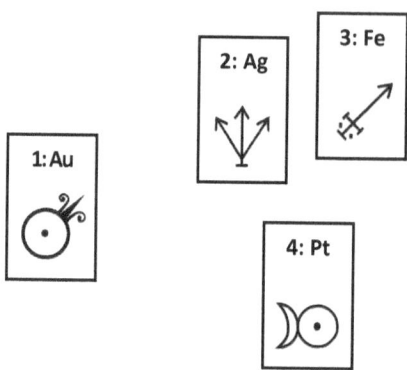

Note from the author of this spread about the translation:

Why translate my spreads to Spanish? I am bilingual and learned both English and Spanish almost simultaneously. The predominant culture around me was influenced by Catholicism but also by magical realism. Combining all of that with being a visual learner makes loving tarot come as no surprise for me. By translating these spreads to Spanish, I am honoring an important part of my roots and communicating these tarot tools to a wider audience. In my translation I use the gender neutral "e" ending for pronouns or words indicating the user's gender. This practice is gaining recognition and usage, particularly among queer folks. It's not easy to change a language like Spanish, which is rigidly structured along the gender binary. As a genderqueer person, I am more than happy to change things to suit queer folks' needs. Language is our tool and should not be our dictator.

THE FOUR METALLIC RULES SPREAD

Sonya Miranda

Most people are familiar with the Golden Rule. Through my work recovering from codependency, I learned of other metallic rules. (from the facilitator of a codependency class I took a few years ago). I've created some prompts based on each rule. Feel free to tailor the prompts for your own situation and based on how these rules apply to your life.

Card 1: The Golden Rule
(Do unto others as you would have them do to you.)
* Where or in what way can I embody my best self?
* How can I be more mindful in how I treat others?

Card 2: The Silver Rule
(Do for yourself what you do for others.)
* How can I take better care of myself?
* How might I be neglecting my own needs while centering others' needs?

Card 3: The Iron Rule
(Don't do for others what they can do for themselves.)
* Where in my life am I crossing other's boundaries and enabling dependence?
* Where can I let go of controlling behaviors?

Card 4: The Platinum Rule
(Love yourself the way you want others to love you.)
* What is preventing me from loving myself?
* What may be forcing me to focus on others rather than myself? How can I heal wounds / build a deep well of self love?

LA TIRADA DE LAS CUATRO REGLAS METÁLICAS

(Traducción por Sonya Miranda)

La mayoría de las personas han oído de la regla de oro. A través de mi recuperación de la codependencia, aprendí de las otras reglas metálicas. No sé quién es ele autore de estas reglas, pero el profesor de la clase de codependencia nos las enseñó. He creado algunas indicaciones basadas en cada regla. Adapta las indicaciones a tu propia situación y en función de cómo se aplican estas reglas a tu vida.

1. La regla de oro: *Trate a les otres como quisieras que te traten a ti.*
* ¿Dónde o de qué manera puedo encarnar mi mejor yo?
* ¿Cómo puedo ser más consciente de cómo trato a les demás?

2. La regla de plata: *Haz por ti misme lo que haces por les demás.*
* ¿Cómo me puedo cuidar mejor?
* ¿Cómo podría estar descuidando mis propias necesidades mientras centro las necesidades de les demás?

3. La regla de hierro: *No hagas por les demás lo que elles pueden hacer por sí mismes.*
* ¿En qué parte de mi vida estoy cruzando los límites de otres y permitiendo la dependencia?
* ¿Dónde puedo dejar de controlar los comportamientos?

4. La regla de platino: *Ámate como quieres que otres te amen.*
* ¿Qué me impide amarme a mí misme?
* ¿Qué puede estar obligándome a centrarme en les demás en lugar de en mí misme?
* ¿Cómo puedo curar heridas y construir un pozo profundo de amor propio?

28

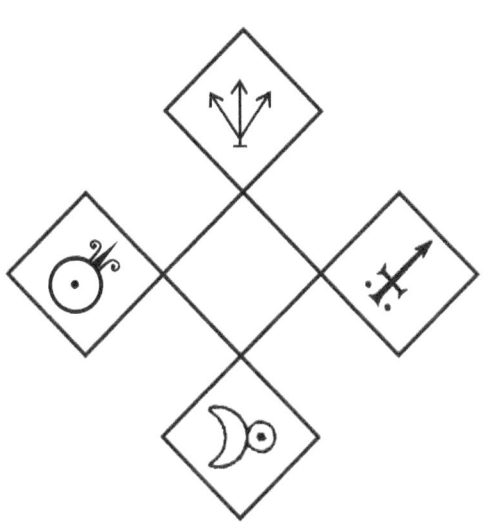

PHONE A FRIEND SPREAD

1	2	3	4	5

PHONE A FRIEND SPREAD

Hannah Kim

Imbue the cards with the energies of your most trusted advisors. Think of an issue you want to address and then call (or txt) your friend and ask them for the following:

1. A number between 1-5. This will be the number of times you shuffle.

2. A number between 1-5. This will be the number of piles you divide your deck into.

3. A random order for the second number they told you (i.e. 2,3,5,4,1 if they gave you 5). This is the order you will put the deck back together in.

4. A number between 1-5. This is the number of cards you will draw.

Draw your card(s). The positional meanings are below. If your friend only has you draw one card, then words of reassurance and encouragement are all you need right now (and so forth).

1. Words of reassurance and encouragement.

2. Advice.

3. What to do about it today (in the present).

4. What to do about it tomorrow (in the future).

5. Lucky card (can mean whenever you need it to mean).

THE LION & THE MOUSE SPREAD

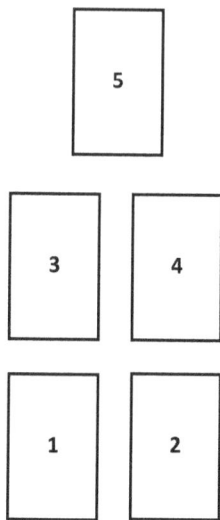

A Lion lay asleep in the forest, his great head resting on his paws. A timid little Mouse came upon him unexpectedly, and in her fright and haste to get away, ran across the Lion's nose. Roused from his nap, the Lion laid his huge paw angrily on the tiny creature to kill her. "Spare me!" begged the poor Mouse. "Please let me go and some day I will surely repay you." The Lion was much amused to think that a Mouse could ever help him. But he was generous and finally let the Mouse go. Some days later, while stalking his prey in the forest, the Lion was caught in the toils of a hunter's net. Unable to free himself, he filled the forest with his angry roaring. The Mouse knew the voice and quickly found the Lion struggling in the net. Running to one of the great ropes that bound him, she gnawed it until it parted, and soon the Lion was free. "You laughed when I said I would repay you," said the Mouse. "Now you see that even a Mouse can help a Lion."

Source: Library of Congress, adapted from the book *The Aesop for Children* published by Rand, McNally & Co in 1919. This work is considered to be in the public domain in the United States.

32

THE LION & THE MOUSE SPREAD

Jen Ciraulo

This spread is based on Aesop's fable "The Lion and the Mouse" and the concept of the Ego. In Western psychology, 'ego strength' refers to a person's capacities for adaptability, cohesive identity, personal resourcefulness, self-efficacy, and self-esteem. An unhealthy ego in psychoanalytic theory is similar to the Eastern concept of an ego, in that the ego is an obstacle in the path to enlightenment, as it is an illusion that keeps us separate from others. In this spread, both things are true, and the path to wholeness is recognition and integration.

1. **Exalted Lion:** Ego Strength: Where one's ego serves the Self.

2. **Ensnared Lion:** Ego Detriment: Where one's ego ensnares the Self.

3. **The Net:** The source of ensnarement.

4. **The Mouse:** Ego Healing/Ego Check: Where one can find balance, humility and freedom in the Self.

5. **Where To Next:** What comes up after integrating these two parts of the Self.

CREATIVE PRACTICE SPREAD

CREATIVE PRACTICE SPREAD

Coleman Stevenson

This spread is for analyzing your creative practice, especially in times when progress feels stalled. I find it helpful to do this both with the cards and with my own rational mind.

First, search for patterns in your work (words, images, themes that repeat across projects). Have you maximized the potential within these personal obsessions? Have they reached the end of usefulness as tropes in your work? Is it time to set them aside and explore new territory?

Next, complete this spread to see if the cards might uncover something you have not noticed. Draw all cards at random:

1. Signifier: Your attitude about your work/process.
2. A tendency in your work that needs to be questioned.
3. A hope for what your work will become or achieve.
4. What to remove.
5. What to add.

4 & 5 may refer to elements of a specific project OR aspects of your creative practice. Define these positions as you wish.

Further cards can be drawn as needed for elaboration/ clarification of any position.

JOE STRUMMER TAROT SPREAD

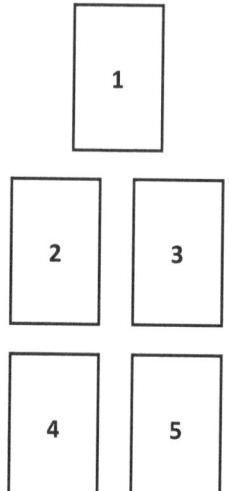

JOE STRUMMER TAROT SPREAD

Liz Worth

We're in a time of uncertainty and upheaval.

Lately, I've been wondering, "What would Joe Strummer do in times like these?" If you're not familiar with the name, Joe Strummer fronted the Clash. The Clash were a pioneering, politically-charged punk band, one that often spoke up for the underdog.

Joe Strummer died on December 22, 2002, at age 50.

Whether you were into punk or not, whether you liked the Clash or not, I feel that Joe Strummer would likely have come out with some wise words to share with the world these days. When I want to connect with his wisdom, I use this tarot spread to see what Joe might have to say about the times we're in:

1. What perspective would Joe Strummer take to help him stay grounded?
2. What message would he share with the public?
3. What action would he take to create change?
4. What action would he encourage you to take?
5. What would he encourage you to create?

ELEMENTAL SPREAD

ELEMENTAL SPREAD

Coleman Stevenson

1. Divide your deck into its five parts— each of the suits and the Major Arcana.

2. Shuffle each pile individually and place it face-down as shown in the diagram: Cups / Pentacles / Swords / Wands / Majors.

3. Turn over the top card in each stack to help determine what needs attention in that elemental realm:

    Cups: Water [Emotional/relational needs]

    Pentacles: Earth [Physical/material needs]

    Swords: Air [Needs in the mental realm/communication]

    Wands: Fire [Needs in the realm of goals and passions]

    Majors: Aether [Needs of the spirit or of the whole self]

VARIATION: Keep a deck divided in this way, left out if you have space for it. Shuffle and draw from any of the elemental piles as needed (rather than drawing one from each) any time you are feeling conflict or confusion in that particular part of yourself.

THE EXPLOSION SPREAD

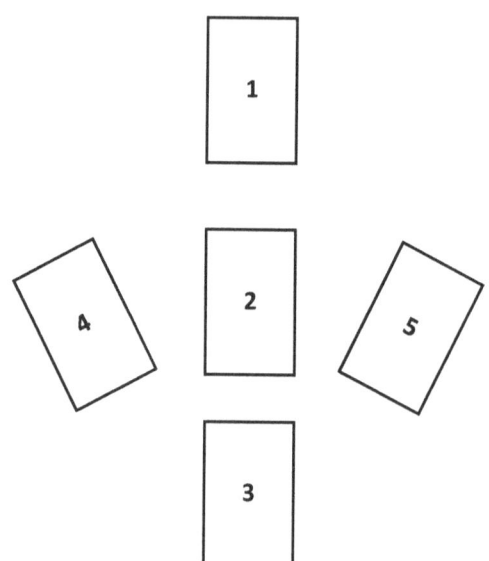

THE EXPLOSION SPREAD

Sir Bran the Blessed

Sometimes, your life seems to fall apart. Nothing seems to make sense anymore, and you feel yourself flayed from the inside out, screaming towards the stars. During these times, I find a blunt and non-bullshit approach is best. This is the type of reader I am and the type of readings I do. Field medicine.

This is the Explosion Spread. It's about how to address a direct problem or set of problems. When I created it, I was dating an extreme addict and I was warring with the fact that unconditional love does not mean unconditional tolerance and lack of boundaries. I had to choose myself. This spread helped me do that.

1. What is your problem?

2. What aren't you facing?

3. What are your first steps?

4. What is your wider challenge?

5. What is your end result?

MANIFESTATION SPREAD FOR LONG-TERM GOALS

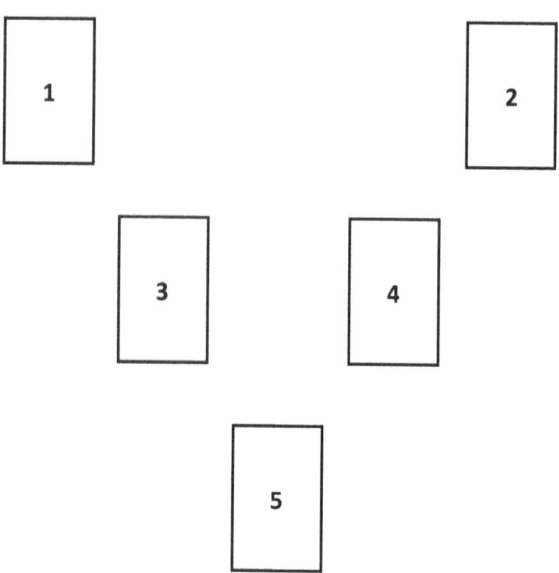

This spread was developed for the New Moon in Capricorn, 2022. Originally for New Year's goal setting, it can be used anytime the following energies are required: **Capricorn** (determination, focus on long-term goals, the value of hard work, laying lasting foundations); **10th House** (ambition and public recognition); **Saturn** (discipline, boundaries, manifestation); **New Moon** (intention-setting, visualization, preparation). Tapping into these energies together can help you understand how best to achieve a long-term goal. Remember that supporting others' goals is as important as supporting your own; you get what you give, but you can only benefit from helping others when coming from an honest, free, and compassionate place.

MANIFESTATION SPREAD FOR LONG-TERM GOALS

Ann Seletos

1. What aspect of my goal(s) needs focus and attention?
2. How can I support others' goals?
3. How can I be more disciplined?
4. What boundaries will support me?
5. What will my commitment to my goals bring in 6 months?*

*For undesirable, or perceived "negative" outcomes for Card 5, consider the following, and pull clarifying cards as needed:

New Levels, New Devils – This may actually be a message of success! But, as the saying goes, once you've achieved a new level, you'll be presented with new challenges. It's a sign of growth and development, and your guides may be indicating what challenges will come after achieving a new status.

Clarity or Healing Around a Current Struggle – If the card reflects a challenge you're currently experiencing, this could indicate overcoming the obstacle or healing that part of the self by the indicated time, especially if the card is reversed.

Adjust Your Intention – You may need to adjust your intention and build a foundation that is in alignment with your most loving and compassionate heart. Does your goal have more to do with materialistic gain or recognition? It doesn't mean you can't have these things, or that wanting them is bad! It's simply important to connect with *why* you want them. For example, if your intention comes from a place of feeling unworthy or inadequate, or feeling the need to prove yourself, your plans will take root in these energies. Take time to realign your intentions from a place of self-love—the seed from which all will grow.

EXPLORING COLOR WITH THE TAROT

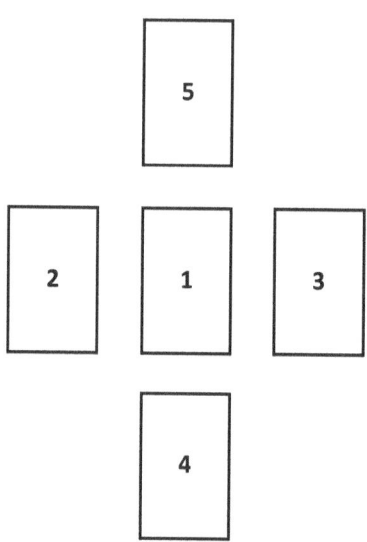

*This method can be layered over any spread. The example spread here is one I use the most for general "weather report" type readings. It's a five card spread, with one card in the center and a card on each side. It's the same as a past, present, and future spread but with lower and higher selves added vertically to the center card. All five cards should form a cross.

EXPLORING COLOR WITH THE TAROT

Greg Traw

Color is an often ignored element in the Tarot, but it's as important as title, number, symbol, and meaning. A well-created deck is conscious and intentional with its color palettes. And with the greatest ones, color becomes a character or narrative on its own. There's a poetry to it. More often than not, I react first to the colors of a card or group of cards and how they interact with each other. Sometimes when experimenting, I'll even make a rule for myself to only use the Tarot for its colors, stripping it of all its form, tradition, and literary influence. Since this is more of an exercise or practice for connecting with a deck, it should probably only be used when working with the cards by yourself.

Start by shuffling the deck as you normally would, draw the first card and place it in the center.* Immediately flip the card over and ignore all elements in the card except the colors. What color or colors jump out at you the most? Commit those to memory. More often than not, one or more colors in the initial card come into consciousness, but at times a totally different color not in the card can manifest. Always go with your intuition. This takes a bit of practice to deprogram yourself from automatically reading the title, number or taking your cues from the images, but that's exactly what this method is meant to do. Cover up any text if you need to. It might be easier to start with a deck with simple color palettes (fewer choices) like the Marseilles and, as you progress, use decks with more complex color. The Thoth Tarot, Fountain Tarot, and Margarete Petersen Tarot are all decks I use when strictly working with color.

Once the color or colors are set to memory, shuffle the deck again. When you're ready, start flipping cards — face up — off the top of the deck. Flip them fast like flash cards. Again by only using color, pull the first card that best represents your selected color(s) and put it into the past position. (You will be surprised how often the first card pulled off the deck is the "right" card.) Now take in how the two cards' colors are interacting with each other. There should be distinct color relationships between the two. At times they can be complimentary while other times they can clash and be opposites. Close your eyes and meditate on them if you need to. What past feelings and associations do they bring up? Deny nothing.

Same as before, commit a color or colors to memory, shuffle and flip the cards over again. Once you found your next card, put it in the future position. Continue to repeat this process with the lower self below the center card and the high self above it. Each time you draw a card you should have its positional meaning's intention in mind, acting as a loose subconscious guide.

Once the spread is complete, pull back and take a macro view of all the colors. There will be pronounced relationships between all of them. There should be a bunch of inspiration with which to interpret them as well. Like a Piet Mondrian painting, see the spread as a whole composition of color. They should tell a story all on their own. You can stop there if the insights are clear enough or start bringing in the other elements in the cards if need be. Often times I will compare and contrast what came up for me as color and what came up as far as the traditional images, symbols, and meanings go. Color is such a subjective experience, often times it adds another layer of subtext to the cards depending on their order or position. The key is to experiment and explore.

46

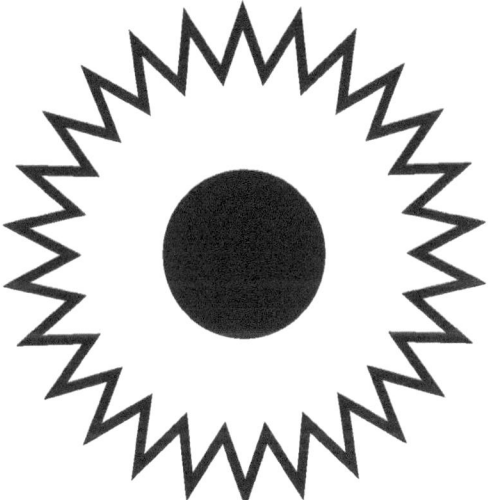

6-CARD SPREAD FOR A LOVERS YEAR

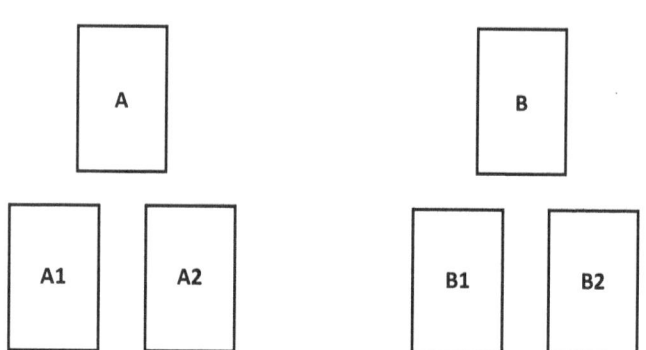

6-CARD SPREAD FOR A LOVERS YEAR

Roberta Aylward

A tarot spread for a year generally or personally associated with Arcanum 6: The Lovers.*

Locate **The Lovers** and **The Devil** cards in your deck and place them face-up on the left and right. Shuffle and draw the remaining cards, placing two underneath The Lovers and two below The Devil. The inquiry for each of the 4 cards (left to right) will be as follows:

A. The Lovers
1. In this moment what deep longing wishes to be tended?
2. How can I nourish this longing?

B. The Devil
1. What is repressing my deepest longing?
2. What practice can I use to support restoration?

*In general, this is any calendar year with numbers adding up to 6 (2022: 2+0+2+2=6). A personal year card is determined by adding your month and day of birth to the current year (in single digits) and reducing until you arrive at a number corresponding with a Major Arcana card.

The Devil, Arcanum 15, can also be reduced to 6 (1+5).

THE CROSSROADS

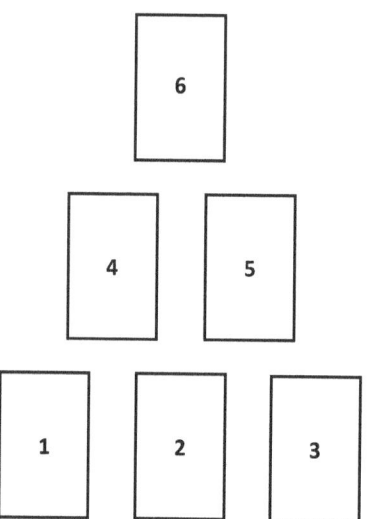

THE CROSSROADS

Corey Coppola

This tarot spread is used to determine next moves, especially in moments when the path is divided before you. I learned the basics of this traditional spread from my family and have adapted it for personal use over time. I recommend using it with **Major Arcana only** and reading **all cards upright** (no reversals).

Cards 1-3: These cards together determine the direction to head at this crossroads. Read them left to right like a sentence. If this answer feels clear and satisfying, the reading can conclude. If this answer feels unclear or problematic, draw cards 4-6 to reveal deeper aspects of the choice or a possible alternate route.

Card 4: Read this in relation to cards 1 and 2.

Card 5: Read this in relation to cards 2 and 3.

Card 6: A final thought connecting these new sentences.

THE CROWN SPREAD

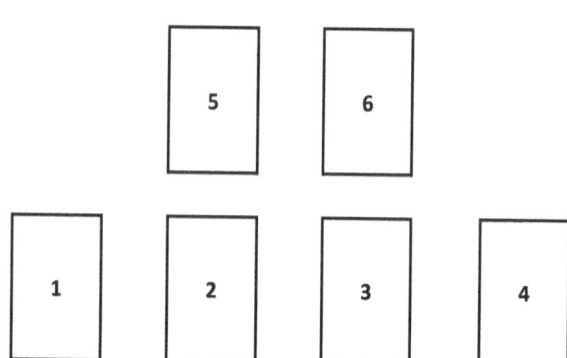

THE CROWN SPREAD

Cherri Roden

For bossing up and taking on self-limiting thoughts.

Read the cards as follows:

1. What thoughts are tethering me to an untruth about myself?

2. How are those thoughts impacting my life?

3. What inner conflict do these thoughts reveal?

4. What does my heart tell me as I face these thoughts?

5. What if I turned these thoughts upside down? What if the opposite were actually real?

6. What truth shines through? What have I learned about these thoughts to help break their hold?

THE WILL TO OVERCOME

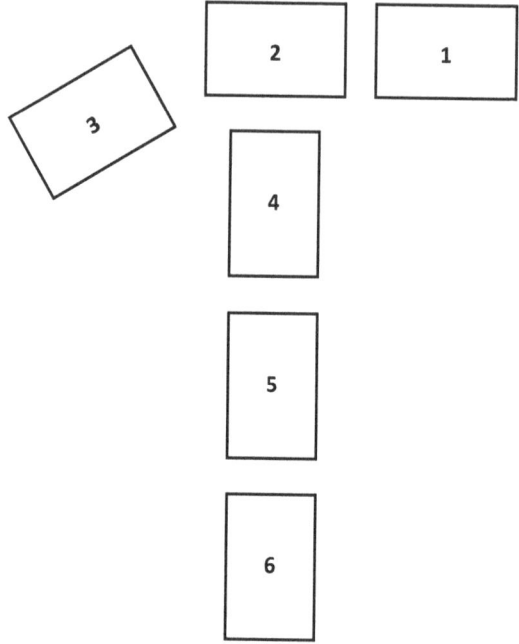

This spread is inspired by the 1914-1916 journey of Ernest Shackleton and the crew of the *Endurance*, a ship that was crushed by ice during an expedition to Antarctica. For 127 days, the 28 men of the *Endurance* survived living on floating ice as it melted away under their feet. It's hard to fathom that in an environment so harsh, no one died. They overcame impossible odds— odds few could imagine enduring. It is hard not to think that only happened because of sheer will, of their collective need to see home again.

THE WILL TO OVERCOME

Leah Sottile

One of the Shackleton crew's only tools was a carpenter's adze, and this spread takes inspiration from both that tool and the modern mountaineering axe: a critical instrument of survival.

This is a spread to be conducted when a problem eats at a person. This spread asks the querent to dig deeply to identify a problem, unearthing it from the root in order to understand it. Then, the spread offers solutions for moving forward, finding new balance and new ways of thinking to stay grounded.

Lay out all cards, and turn over each one in numerical order. Upon arriving at the sixth position, flip the card. If it is not a major arcana card, continue to draw from the deck until you arrive at one.

1. **The Adze:** The digging that needs to be done; the thing to unearth.

2. **The Head:** The thought to discard.

3. **The Pick:** A rule to break.

4. **The Leash:** A lifeline in this process.

5. **The Shaft:** A place of balance.

6. **The Spike:** Plant this firmly into the ground to move forward.

THE LEGALIS* SPREAD

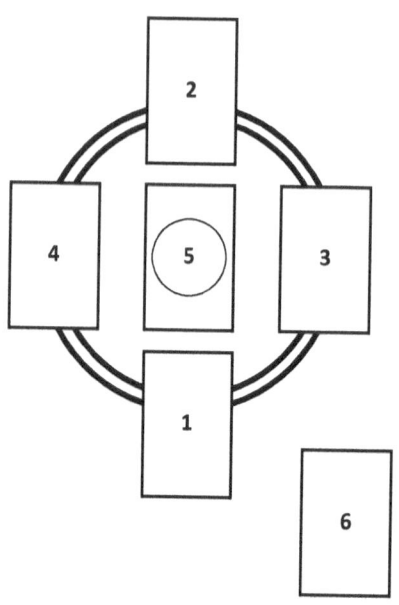

A note about this spread from its creator:

When I feel an injustice has occurred or I am seeking clarity and perspective regarding certain circumstances, I go to my tarot and state my claim. It reduces my stress because I don't feel like a victim anymore. I've turned the matter over to higher courts that may shed light on the matter, helping me consider it in a different, more peaceful way.

*The word *legal* is derived from the Latin *legalis*.

**Edicts are proclamations passed down from a higher authority.

56

THE LEGALIS SPREAD

Melanie Trowbridge

In this spread we are asking for Natural Law Edicts** and communications from The Great Beyond / our intuitive Higher Selves. Matters can range from seemingly trivial to that of great importance. You are asking that attention be brought forth to an injustice. Therefore, state your case truthfully, plainly, and with factual evidence prior to beginning. Ensure you are ready for guidance and a ruling to follow. Ask for the spread to operate from the side of Justice, a place of loving kindness and greater understanding. As you begin with the card for "That Which Grounds," it may be helpful to imagine grounding in your own body, such as rooting or feeling connection to the Earth. Proceed through the positions as numbered. Take a moment to prepare yourself before revealing the Edict card to evaluate any personal responsibility in the matter.

1. **That Which Grounds:** What gives the quest its roots and ensures stability in the questioner.

2. **That Which Rises:** A more Universal perspective; distance that reveals connections of all paths.

3. **That Which Empowers:** What gives the questioner agency, assistance, or guidance towards a more balanced situation.

4. **That Which Sustains:** The long-term needs of the journey; what nourishes and supports a pathway to its completion.

5. **The Center Point:** What everything revolves around, the crux of the matter, or why the situation may have occurred in the first place.

6. **The Final Edict:** A decree issued providing guidance.

ASSERTIVENESS SPREAD

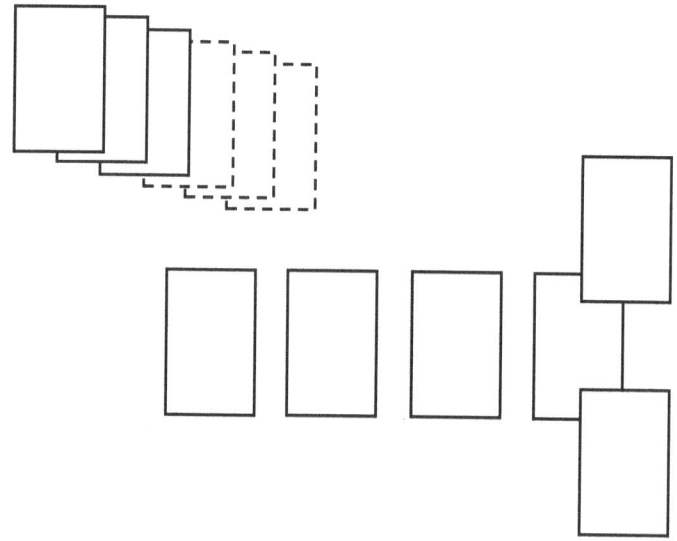

See a note from this spread's creator about translation on p. 26.

ASSERTIVENESS SPREAD

Sonya Miranda

Expressing needs, boundaries, and desires is incredibly important. As someone who is codependent, expressing those needs assertively is very difficult. I find that I am assertive in some situations and not in others. This spread is meant to help you identify situations in which you could be more assertive.

Take charge of the spread—the cards don't have to fall where they want, but where YOU want.

1. Pick 3 to 6 cards.

2. Turn them over and analyze how each one represents a situation in your life, and whether you assert your needs, wants, and boundaries in those situations.

3. Determine which situations you tend to be the least assertive in. Put your cards in order from left to right with left being most assertive, and right being the least assertive situations.

4. Draw two more cards for your least assertive situation.

   a. Top card: Where can I find the strength to better express this need?

   b. Bottom card: How will my life change if I start expressing this need?

Repeat this step as desired for the other cards.

TIRADA DE ASERTIVIDAD

(Traducción por Sonya Miranda)

Expresar necesidades, límites y deseos es increíblemente importante. Como alguien que es codependiente, expresar asertivamente esas necesidades es muy difícil. Encuentro que soy asertive en algunas situaciones, y no en otras. Esta tirada está diseñada para ayudarte a identificar situaciones en las que podrías ser más asertive.

Hágase cargo de la tirada, las cartas no tienen que caer donde ellas quieran, sino donde TÚ quieras.

1. Escoja 3 a 6 cartas.

2. Analiza cómo cada carta representa situaciones en tu vida y en cuanto afirmas tus necesidades y derechos en esas situaciones.

3. Determina el orden de las cartas descendiendo de más a menos asertividad.

4. Escoja dos cartas más para la situación de menos asertividad.

   a. Para la carta de arriba: ¿Cual es mi fuente de fortaleza para mejor afirmar esta necesidad?

   b. Para la carta de abajo: ¿Cómo va a cambiar mi vida si empiezo a afirmar mis necesidades mejor?

   Repita con las otras cartas.

CHAKRA SPREAD

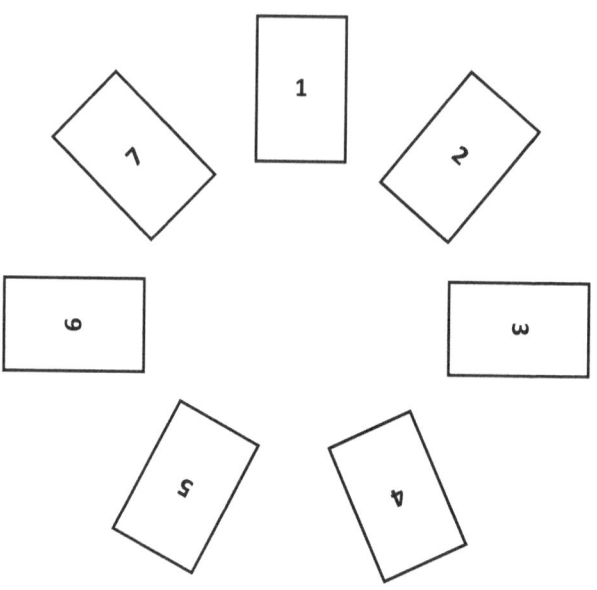

Chakras can serve as a representation of the right/ability to:

> Be/Take space
> Feel/Desire
> Act/Create
> Love/Connect
> Speak/Give voice
> See/Intuit
> Deeply know/Connect to our wisest, most compassionate self/the Whole/Universe/Spirit/etc.

For this spread, we use a question to explore each Chakra in general or in relation to a specific area in life.

CHAKRA SPREAD

Skylar Haven

The Spread

Draw 7 cards however you like to draw them and lay them out in a circle. If you are following the hours of the clock, it works out to be a card around 12:00, 1:30, 3:00, 4:30, 7:30, 9:00, and 10:30. For each position there's a question to reflect on:

1. Where am I drawing my value / enoughness from?
2. What do I need to allow myself to feel or desire right now?
4. What needs to change around what I'm doing/not doing?
5. What does my heart want me to know?
6. What truth do I need to speak?
7. What do I (need to) see clearly?
8. What's a wise and compassionate next step?

Affirmations (Optional)

When you have explored the answers that arise to these questions, you might go back around the circle and speak an affirmation. Here are examples to start with:

1. I am enough and allowed to take up space.
2. My desires and feelings are welcome and offer valuable direction.
3. I choose to engage in tangible ways / My actions connect to the inner and outer worlds.
4. I honor my heart and the heart of others.
5. My voice is important, I give voice to my truths.
6. I mindfully look to see more clearly.
7. With wisdom and compassion I take a next step.

TAPE DECK SPREAD

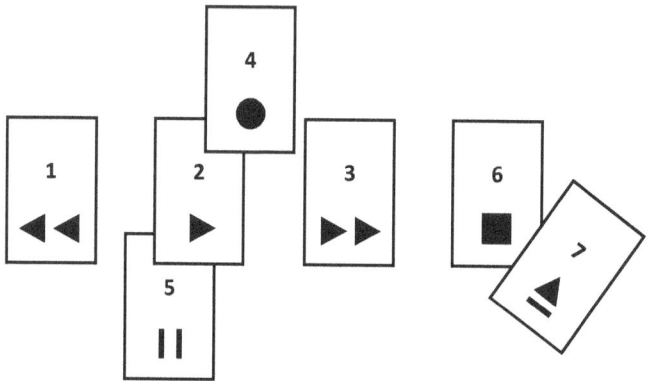

TAPE DECK SPREAD

Lars Sparby

This spread is a machine for telling and retelling stories. It's an automatic magical collage device. It emulates a physical object that's now already become an arcane and obsolete form of technology: the tape deck. A Tarot deck in and of itself might very well be described as an arcane form of technology, much, much older than the one previously mentioned, yet it is by no means obsolete. But is it in danger of becoming outdated? That's probably something you could go ahead and ask the cards themselves if you really want to know the answer. However, just to be on the safe side, we should continue to deconstruct and dream up different ways to interface with the Arcana. I deeply believe it's our sacred duty as creative cartomancers to think outside of the box and to play with convention.

1. **REWIND: Past.** What you need to go back to and examine in greater detail.

2. **PLAY: Present.** What's currently playing. The stuff that's going on in your life right now.

3. **FAST FORWARD: Future.** Move towards this... or where things are headed if you don't follow the instructions suggested from positions 4, 5, 6 and 7.

4. **RECORD: Tape over this.** What you you should replace. Relates to the PLAY card position.

5. **PAUSE: Put this on hold.** What you need a break from.

6. **STOP: Stop doing this.** This has to stop.

7. **EJECT: Reject.** What to let go of and leave behind.

MODES OF OPERATION

At first glance, this may not look like anything other than an extended play on the traditional, tried and tested Past-Present-Future classic spread. And to some extent, that's true, because it can simply function as just that. However, there are two distinct modes of operation:

Mode One: The first mode is to just use it as a slightly more in-depth Past-Present-Future variation.

Mode Two: The second mode is when it becomes more interesting. In this mode, we suppose that once something has been recorded, it can be played back, and not only that, once recorded, it can be   edited. What does that mean exactly? Well, it means that you can "play back" previous reads you have done in the past. Therefore, you can use this layout as a method to not only insert prior three-card "recordings" but also to revisit reads you've done with this particular spread itself. Things can get even more interesting if you decide to either use a different deck than you did last time or multiple decks simultaneously by laying new cards on top of the old ones. This last approach will add intriguing layers of interpretation.

REMIXING

The accompanying sequence of button/card positions is a carefully chosen alchemical formula that has been arrived upon after a lot of experimentation. That being said, feel free to play around with the arrangement and remix in your own experiments, as this can make the experience vastly more exciting.

LIVE THROUGH THIS SPREAD

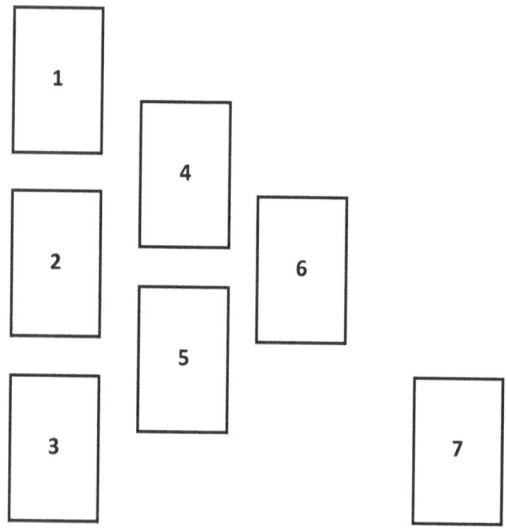

LIVE THROUGH THIS SPREAD
A spread for challenging times.

Jen Ciraulo

This spread can be used for any difficult life circumstance, situation, or time period according to the following instructions.

Step 1: Separate Major Arcana, Court Cards, and Minor Arcana.

Step 2: Shuffle Minors and draw cards 1, 2, and 3. Read top to bottom, these cards address the question: What can I do to make it through?

* Card 1: Primary focus/most helpful advice,
* Card 2: Secondary level of importance/focus on next,
* Card 3: Lowest priority but still helpful and relevant.

Step 3: Shuffle Court Cards and draw cards 4 and 5. Also consider how you can integrate the these two aspects of the self to promote a sense of health and authenticity.

* Card 4: What can I embody or focus on internally that will offer strength and support?
* Card 5: How can I navigate my outer life most skillfully?

Step 4: Shuffle Majors and draw card 6.

* Card 6: What can I learn from this experience? How can this experience help me grow as a person?

Step 5: Shuffle all the remaining cards and draw one final card:

* Card 7: PS Card/Food for thought. What comes up here can offer clarity and a final word.

HARMONY IN OPPOSITION

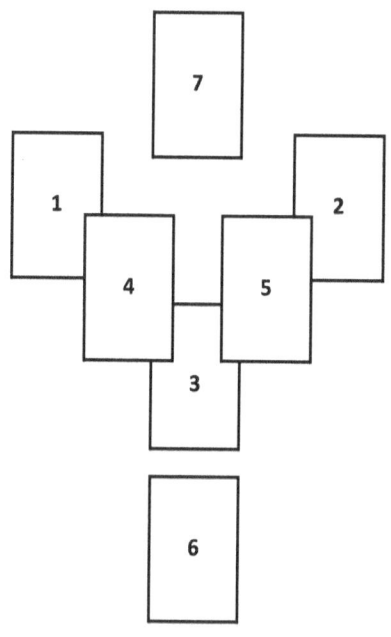

HARMONY IN OPPOSITION

Charlie Claire Burgess

Use this spread when you're having a hard time reconciling two seemingly opposing things in your life. These may be two conflicting areas of life, such as making art and making a paycheck; two warring desires, such as craving excitement but also safety; two contrary parts of yourself, such as your head and your heart; two parties in an argument; or any other pairing that has you divided.

So often the things we assume to be binary and irreconcilable are anything but. Musical harmony requires different notes, after all, and balance is not a state of sameness but of the constant, fluid adjustments between extremes. Sometimes we just need a little help seeing beyond the binary.

1 + 2.   Two opposing things in your life.

3.   What they have in common.

4.   What 1 can learn from 2.

5.   What 2 can learn from 1.

6.   What you can learn from their relationship.

7.   How to find harmony and balance.

SPREAD FOR THE SNOW MOON

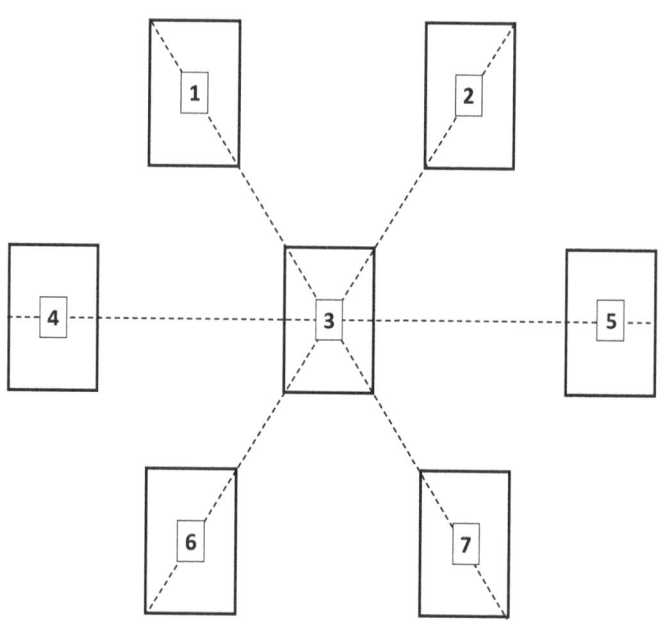

SPREAD FOR THE SNOW MOON

Cherri Roden

...or any time you're feeling cold, detached or uninspired. The Snow Moon appears in February, as that is typically the snowiest month of the year in northern North America.

Read the cards as follows:

The cold...

1. Where have I become cold, detached, uninspired?

2. How is the chill impacting me?

3. What has brought the cold?

The blanket...

4. How do I care for myself in this awareness?

5. What is a source of joy, beauty, or magic I can tap into for warmth?

The fire...

6. What change(s) can I make to spark inspiration? What can melt my heart?

7. How do I keep the fire burning?

BUSINESS TAROT SPREAD

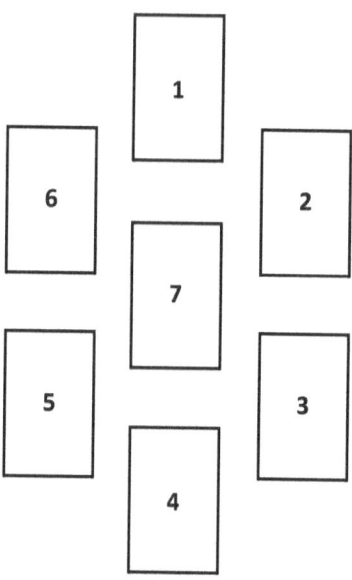

BUSINESS TAROT SPREAD

Zoë Torres

1. What have you overcome to get where you are now?

2. How do you currently feel about your business?

3. How are you approaching the management of your finances?

4. What is something you offer that has inherent value?

5. What are you calling in at the moment?

6. What is ready for change, overhaul, update, upgrade?

7. How are your clients & customers impacted by your work?

SOME ANAGOGIC ORACLE ABOUT ASTOUNDING FORESHADOWING

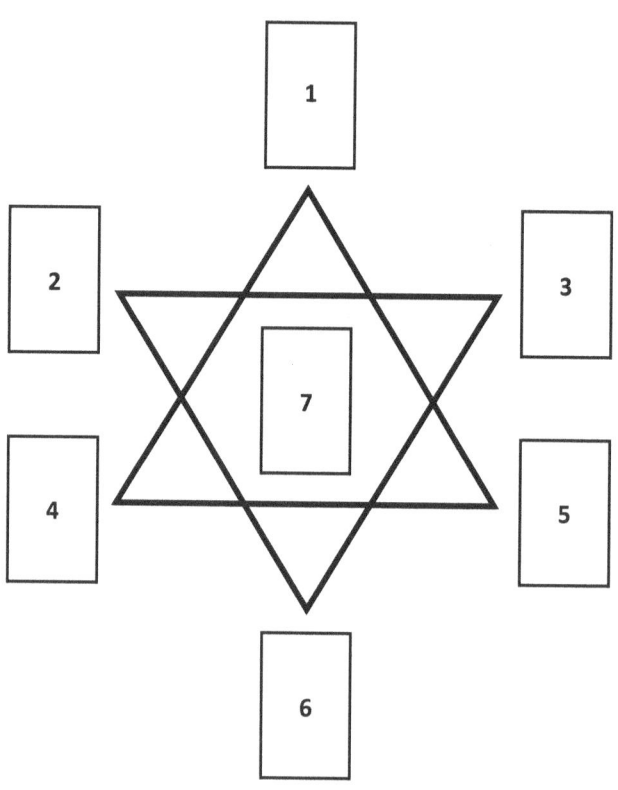

This spread was crafted using THE RANDOM ESOTERIC SPREAD THINGAMAGIG found on p. xxiii.

SOME ANAGOGIC ORACLE ABOUT ASTOUNDING FORESHADOWING

Lars Sparby

Card meanings:

1. Who you really are in this scenario.

2. Why you shouldn't care.

3. Why the time is right.

4. Why you shouldn't care.

5. Why you should care.

6. Where to investigate further.

Twist:

7. A new piece of evidence that may change everything.

TRIANGLE OF MANIFESTING SPREAD

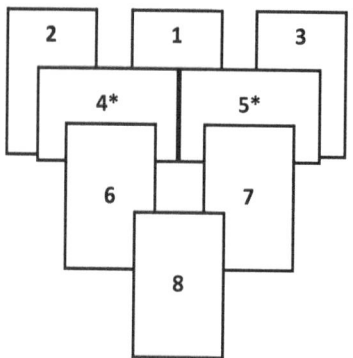

*Note from the spread creator:

I read a card turned toward the right as upright, while a card that is turned left represents a lean towards the reverse meaning of the card.

TRIANGLE OF MANIFESTING SPREAD

Via Hedera

Shuffle the deck and cut in three. Restack in any intuited order.

The theme of this reading is to follow down the left or the right side of the upside-down triangle created by the spread. It is meant for each path to be read alternately, giving insight into how both action or conflict and peace (or at least, passiveness) will guide you through a dilemma. The point of reading the cards in alternating order (left, then right, then left, etc.) until the last card is to always remind the self to read an issue in a balanced way; give consideration to both sides of the coin at every turn.*

Card 1. The Central Issue: The heart of a particular problem that has recently arisen or is soon to unfold.

Card 2. Left Hand/The Path of Conflict: If you pursue an active or warrior's stance in this issue, what will this manifest as?

Card 3. Right Hand/The Path of Passivity: On the other hand, if you take a path of peace or passiveness, what will this manifest as?

Cards 4 & 5. The Bridge Between Paths (to be read in conjunction): This bridge tells of a connection between the hearts of the issues, and how conflict will connect to peace.

Card 6. The Outcome of the Left Path: What will likely unfold should you follow this path to its natural conclusion. Sometimes confrontation and conflict are growing tools, necessities of life, and can lead to better places than passiveness would have.

79

Card 7. The Outcome of the Right Path: What will unfold should you follow this path to its natural conclusion. Sometimes, a path of least resistance and temperance is needed to approach a situation, to tame an unnecessary conflict.

Card 8. A Piece of Advice: The final card is the advice of the spread, accounting for all previous cards as they follow down both the left and the right-hand paths. It is not a result card, it is a word of wisdom that can be applied to each side of the coin. If I follow the path of conflict, what should I bear in mind as I move down it? If I choose the clockwise path, what should I consider and how does this card apply to my scenario? Sometimes all it takes is a final word of wisdom to shape one's choices, change one's path.

FALLEN STAR SPREAD

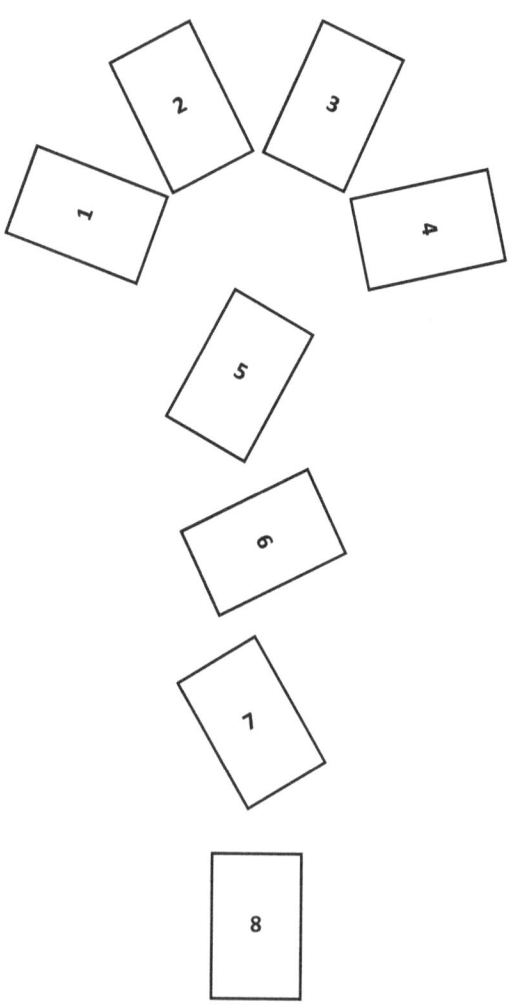

FALLEN STAR SPREAD

Joseph O'Sullivan

A spread for when everything seems out of control— eight cards derived from the uncanny process.*

Read the cards in the following contexts:

1. **The Constellation:** The place/role that you're used to.

2. **Deep, Dark Space:** What you fear beyond your field of vision.

3. **The Order of the Universe:** The rules you've lived by.

4. **The Fall:** What to consider amid a loss of control.

5. **Trajectory:** What to give up OR focus on amid this journey. (Card reader's choice: choose *give up* or choose *focus*, or let the card as placed determine which.)

6. **Friction/Heat:** What to consider amid uncomfortable feelings/ strange new energy.

7. **Reposition:** How to best prepare for what you face next.

8. **Impact:** Lessons learned through loss of control.

*See p. xx-xxii.

RECOVERY/RECLAIMING SPREAD

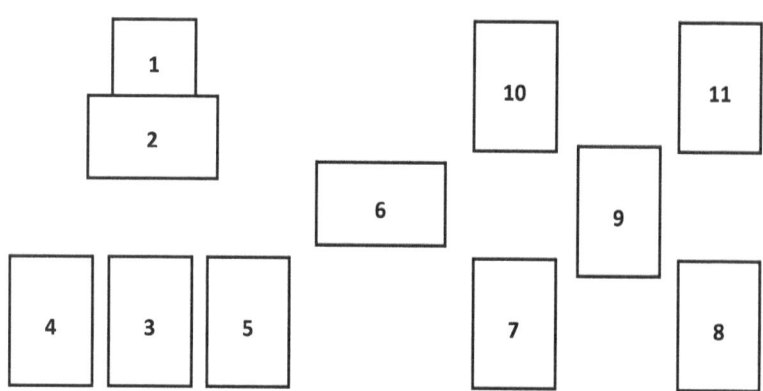

A note about this spread from its creator:

I conceived of this layout as both a way to make sense of my own recovery journey, as well as offer it to others who are struggling. There is always more to know and discover about oneself in relation to getting over an addiction. My own demon was alcohol, but this spread can be used for any number of other addictions that land us with a monkey on our back.

RECOVERY/RECLAIMING SPREAD

Juanita Esperanto

1. **Significator:** An archetypal energy. Who you are right now in your recovery journey. How you are showing up in the world.

2. **Crossing Card:** Forces outside your control that may be for or against you. Blend this card's energy with Card 1.

3. **The self in this moment:** The self you're presenting or performing. (True self struggling for sobriety, recovery, redemption OR the oppressor self.)

4. **Context/Environment:** The background from which the addiction or the desire to give it up emerged. Also, the context around using. This is an important card/energy for the querent to remember.

5. **Past < and Future >:** The position of this card represents a double-edged sword. This card is the split, the unsustainable influences, the exact point that determines you can no longer stay where you are nor can you let go of it. Where you are being torn in two.

6. **Bridge to Recovery:** How you got there.

7. **Work:** The ground you are building or gaining.

8. **The Ground You Are Losing:** Forces that are antagonistic to your recovery process.

9. **The Moment of Surrender.**

10. **Response to the Outcome:** Where you're at once it all settles down.

85

RETRATO ASTRAL SPREAD

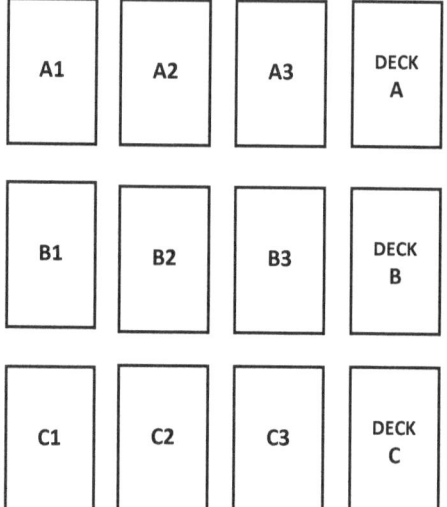

RETRATO ASTRAL SPREAD

Alan Pérez

The Retrato Astral ("Stellar Portrait") reading uses three distinct types of decks:

* an astrology oracle deck (In the deck I use I omitted the moon phase cards, but that is a choice each can make.)

* a Tarot deck (Waite/Smith, Thoth or any of style of your choice)

* and a Lenormand deck

This spread is modeled after a Lenormand portrait spread using a grid of 3x3. However, each row is a different deck. Shuffle all three decks and cut them. Draw three cards from each, laying them out according to the diagram. Place the remainder of each deck at the end of its respective row, turned over so that the bottom card now faces up.

Deck A is the astrology oracle. Its position here represents the 'as above" perspective in the esoteric dictum "as above, so below," as the zodiac represents a larger clock influencing daily experiences.

Deck B is the Tarot deck. It will provide advice and guidance for the overall theme of the spread.

Deck C is a Lenormand deck. It is the "so below" continuation to the decks above it. This row is a real-time understanding of the material world as it is playing out around you.

You can read each column as 2-3 days prior (left), present (center), and 2-3 days into the future (right). The overall theme of the spread is a reading of the three upward-facing cards in the right column.

WAY OF THE FOOL

WAY OF THE FOOL

Stephanie Adams-Santos

A personal ritual reading for self-improvement and reflection.

> "Sleep, soft smiling, draws me unto her: and those receive me, who quietly treat me, as one familiar and well-beloved in that home: but will not, oh, will not, not now, not ever; but will not ever tell me who I am."
>
> – James Agee

This quote by James Agee comes from *Knoxville: Summer of 1915*, a 16-minute dramatic song for soprano and orchestra. No matter how many times I encounter these words, the power of its assertion wrecks me anew: nobody, not even our most familiar and beloved, can tell us who we are. It's a question we can only truly approach by confronting again and again and again in small solitary glimpses the unwieldy mystery of what we are.

I created this reading as a ritual for tender self-examination and inquiry towards a better understanding of ourselves at the moment of the reading. Involved here is an implicit prayer or calling of grace: May I always evolve toward the best version of myself; may I be unafraid of my own reflections and shadows; may I continue to grow into a version of myself I can love and be proud of. By taking on this reading with honesty and openness, you invoke these blessings in your journey.

Instructions

For this reading you will ideally need **two decks**, though it can be done with one by omitting the ritual aspect of the reading. The **first deck** should be your most charged and potent deck, one whose images are especially moving and powerful to you.

The **second deck** can be any trustworthy reading deck. For Tarot experts, try to use a second deck that you haven't used in a long time, or perhaps a more unfamiliar deck to heighten and encourage the energy of the Fool.

Set the stage for your ritual. Gather a cloth, candle, incense and/or any ritual objects that help represent how you would like to evolve. For example, some of the items I like to use for this ritual are my brass scorpion to remind me of my fixed cosmic elements, and a small bowl of water with a glass eye at the bottom to remind me of vision that comes through a balance of stillness, motion, and mystery.

From the first deck, remove the **Fool** and **World** cards from the Major Arcana. Place these about four cards apart, with the Fool on the left in the "starting" position, and the World on the right, in the "finale" position. This represents an arc of transformation:

> **The Fool:** An aspect or version of the Self that is in need of growth or transformation (the immature self)
>
> **The World:** An aspect of the Self that will come to take root after transformation and growth has been achieved (the mature self)

Next, also from the first deck: pull the four Aces from the Minor Arcana and place these in-between the Fool and the World in any order you wish. These represent the following stages of transformation necessary to move between where you are now, and the person you wish to become:

> **Ace of Swords:** An aspect of Self to release or someone/something to make amends with
>
> **Ace of Cups:** A fledgling strength to embrace or a weakness in need of better understanding

Ace of Pentacles: A habit or old wound that needs material attention

Ace of Wands: A vital aspect of life in need of expansion and/or renewal.

These six cards are not just a map of your tarot spread, but an invocation of these cards' highest qualities to strengthen your journey.

For the reading itself, touch the second deck and turn your gaze inward, infusing a still and honest sense of yourself into the cards. Shuffle the cards with this open, self-reflexive energy and, when you are ready, draw the first card from the top and place it above the Fool. Draw the last card at the bottom of the deck and place it above the World. Cut the deck four times, each time drawing the top card to place above the four Aces.*

Read left to right, first examining the arc of transformation as a whole, and then in its individual stages. The key to this ritual is to approach it with radical honesty and compassion. In the spirit of the Fool, be open to surprises and to seeing yourself in a new way.

As closure to your reading ritual, craft a brief personal mantra or wish from what the cards have revealed to you. Write this on a small piece of paper and place it in a bowl of water weighted down with a stone. Leave it in a bright place until the water evaporates.

*If using the Dark Exact Tarot as your first deck, you can deepen the reading by adding the Fool Omega after the World card. Draw an additional card from the second deck to place over this one as an indicator of what new journey of growth awaits you.

THE WAY THROUGH

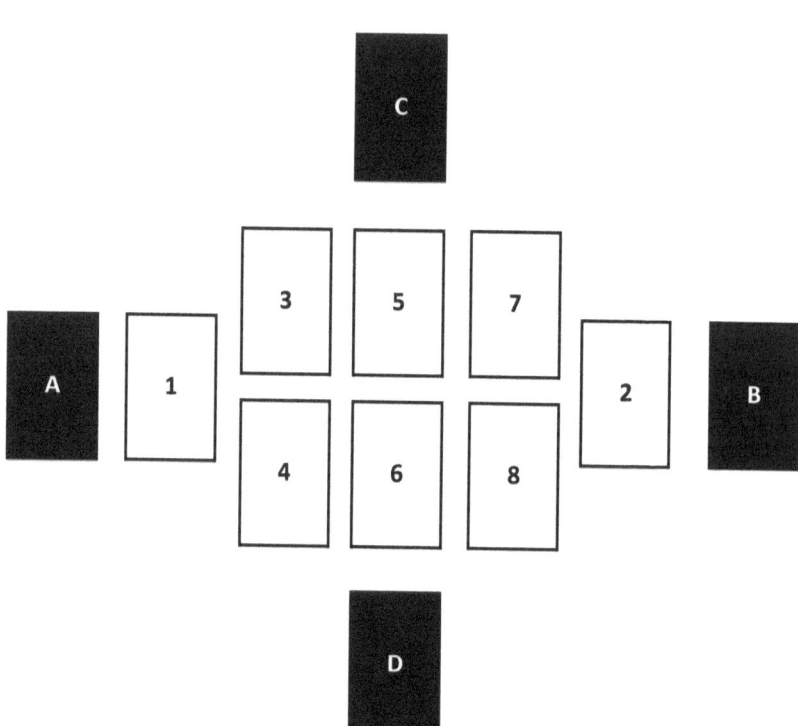

THE WAY THROUGH

Janaki Phillips

This is a tarot spread for uncertain times when the way through a particular situation is unclear; for when the road ahead is dark, and you don't know where the path is leading; or for when you simply cannot imagine a way to get from point A to point B.

Dealing the cards: This spread takes inspiration from earlier practices of tarot reading where the method of dealing out the cards was perhaps as important as the positions in the spread themselves but adds a twist by adding in positions for oracle cards to be read in combination with tarot. I have found that combining tarot and oracle cards can add not only clarification but also offers opportunities for inflection and delightful moments of synchronicity! In this reading, cards A-D are pulled from an oracle deck, and cards 1-8 are pulled from a tarot deck.

When dealing the cards, Card A and Card 1 are dealt from the tops of their respective decks to represent your current situation, and Card B and Card 2 are dealt from the bottoms of the decks to represent where you are headed. Then at the heart of this spread are two three-card readings. The lower row Cards 4, 6, 8, and D) represents the path from your starting point to your destination, and the top row (Cards 3, 5, 7, and C) represents advice on how to navigate the way. Begin dealing these middle cards from the top of their decks as if you were dealing in a person sat across from you in a card game (perhaps a trusted advisor or guide): the first card is dealt away from you, the next one in front of you and so forth, until you have three cards on top and three cards on bottom.

Interpret the cards as follows:

<u>Where you are now</u>: Tarot Card 1 & Oracle Card A
These cards represent where you are at the present moment, your point A, or the starting place from which your next steps will commence.

<u>Where you are headed</u>: Tarot Card 2 & Oracle Card B (dealt from the bottom)
These cards represent where you are headed, your point B, or the destination point of your current endeavor. Remember, as with all "outcome" positions, steps can always be taken to change an undesired result.

<u>Bottom Row</u>: Tarot Cards 4, 6, 8 & Oracle Card D
These four cards represent a way through to your destination. I like to think of them as a practical bridge from point A to point B. You can read these three cards separately as three sequential steps that need to be taken, or together and combine their meanings to create a sentence or an overall picture. The oracle card will provide additional information about your way through.

<u>Top Row</u>: Tarot Cards 3, 5, 7 & Oracle Card C
These four cards represent advice you will need along the way. I like to think of them as the "high road." If the bottom road represents the practical and earthly steps you will need to take, the "high road" represents the spiritual advice or words of guidance you will need to help negotiate your path. You can either read these cards as individual pieces of advice relating to each step of your way or combine their meanings to create a sentence or an overall guiding message. The oracle card will provide additional information about the guidance you will need.

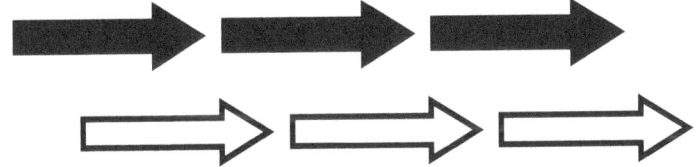

BECOMING THE HAG SPREAD

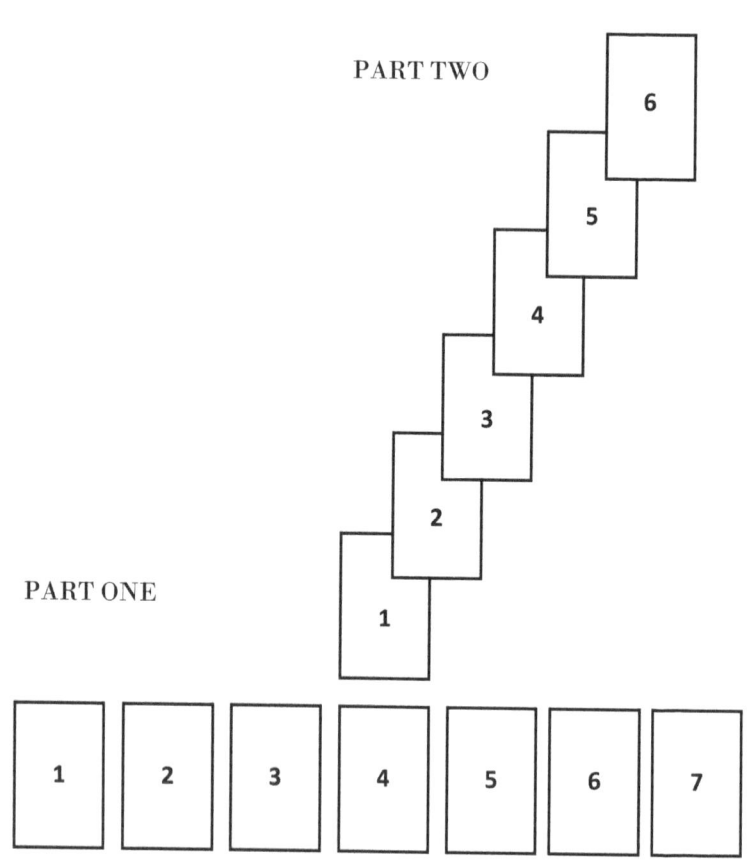

PART TWO

PART ONE

BECOMING THE HAG SPREAD

Natalie Kirby

"And you all know security
Is mortals' chief enemy."
— Hecate, *Macbeth*

"The moon is my mother. She is not sweet like Mary.
Her blue garments unloose small bats and owls"
— *Ariel*, Sylvia Plath

Youth, beauty, fertility, light, and love. These are not the words of the Hag. The Hag is profane and a reject of society. A shriveled womb. The Hag is no one's wife or mother. There's no space for the Hag in the traditional roles of a patriarchal society. The Hag is despised- hated. The Hag is not a Dark Feminine. The Hag is not a feminine at all. The Hag is an incarnation of Nothing and Everything. The Hag is the monster of misogyny, its creation.

The "Glinda" witches have had plenty of spotlight. The stories of witches who use their power to retain physical youth and beauty are tiresome and overplayed. Those are the narratives of the patriarchy. They are small and limited. "As if that's the only purpose of magic and power!" cackles the Hag. The Hag is of a different mind. The power of the Hag has a different purpose— the purpose of knowledge, the purpose of agency, the purpose of Will. The Hag serves only The Hag.

Directions: Read the following spell out loud while shuffling your cards. Once you have finished reading it, lay the cards out according to the diagram, selecting them however you choose.

Become the Hag. Sacrifice your Youth, that Inner Child, and feast with old Kronos. Crack and cackle your eyes into Crows' feet. Greet the Prince of True Will with the Osculum Infame! Become the Hag. Let your skin dry up and shrivel; rub your old naked body with ointments made from the fat of your youth and FLY! Fly and pass through keyholes, door cracks, and chimneys. Become the Hag. Turn your enemy into a pig, and like old Lilith, sit atop and ride your enemy ragged before the break of dawn for no other reason than because you can. Let them wake up hag-ridden, withered, and horrified. Shatter their security. Break their peace. Become the Hag.

PART ONE: To Become the Hag

1. **Child Sacrifice:** This is a part of your identity that you want to "maintain" or keep youthful. It is an expectation you might have for yourself that serves others/society. Kill it. Eat it. Break its bones with your teeth. Tear the sinews. Use its fat for flying ointment.

2. **Crows' Feet:** Where to laugh and accept the parts of yourself that society rejects.

3. ***Osculum Infame:*** "The Shameful Kiss" is an act of degradation and initiation for the witch/hag where they kissed the anus of the Devil. This is how you can learn to bite and become mean and nasty. Dare to take the "low-road" and kiss the ass of the Devil.

4. **Flying Ointment:** What to rub all over your old naked body to fly! This is how to get hag-vision, a needed new perspective that takes you beyond the bounds of ordinary reality. (Not sure how to make your flying ointment? Refer to PART TWO!)

5. **The Keyhole:** What you will need to get through that might SEEM challenging.

6. **Hag-ridden:** How to terrorize your enemies. This is your ability to force others out of their comfort zones.

7. **Becoming the Hag:** Your Highest Hag Potential. This is the Wisdom of the Hag.

PART TWO (Optional)

Flying Ointment Recipe: A getting started/initiative reading. Are you new to flight? Perhaps you're not quite certain how to get off the ground? You need to make some flying ointment, specific to your needs, that will help you to fly.

1. **Fat of the Child:** An attitude or fear to sacrifice and use for fuel.

2. **Belladonna:** A hidden area of ancient inner strength to draw upon.

3. **Mandrake:** New attitude/perspective to help you get off the ground.

4. **Black Henbane:** Preventing motion sickness. A vulnerability to nurture.

5. **Hemlock:** Keeping steady. What needs to be consistently maintained/a habit to develop.

6. **Wolfsbane:** Taking Flight. The moment of initial ascent.

A PERSPECTIVE OF TIME

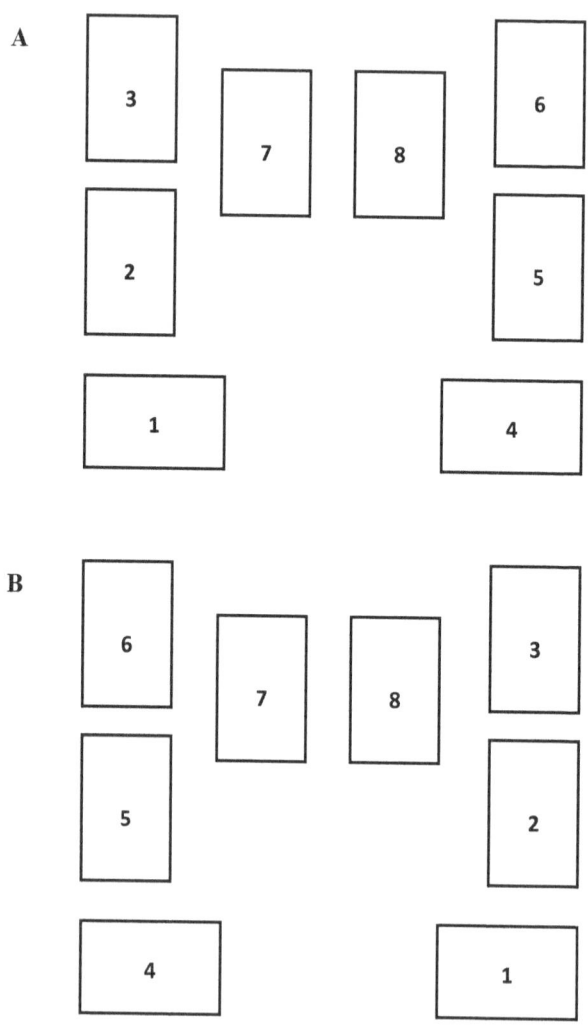

This spread was inspired by the classic Two of Cups card—two people holding goblets toward each other, an expression of joyful union.

A PERSPECTIVE OF TIME

Denise Harwood

This spread has two modes: the querent in the present, interrogating a future self about how to get where they are, OR the querent in the present examining a past self and what trials they overcame to become the person they are now. The first helps examine possibilities when stuck; it's possible to look at the future self presented and reject it. The second is more introspective (*How did I get here?*), which may unlock further avenues of questioning.

A. Present to Future

1: The path you have traveled so far.

2: What you hold in your heart.

3: What you hold in your mind.

4: The path you will have traveled.

5: What you will hold in your heart.

6: What you will hold in your mind.

7: The main problem of the present.

8: How you will solve that problem.

B. Present to Past

1: The path you have traveled.

2: What you hold in your heart.

3: What you hold in your mind.

4: Your circumstances at the start.

5: How your heart was then.

6: How your mind was then.

7: The main problem of the past.

8: How you solved that problem.

INDEX

CONTRIBUTORS

Stephanie Adams-Santos is a Guatemalan-American writer whose work spans poetry, prose, and screenwriting, always with a penchant for the queer and fantastical. She is the author of *Dream of Xibalba* (forthcoming, winner of the Orison Prize in Poetry), *Swarm Queen's Crown* (finalist for the Lambda Literary Awards), *Total Memory*, and *The Sundering* (selected for a New York Chapbook Fellowship by Poetry Society of America). Stephanie has been a story editor on the CW anthology series *Two Sentence Horror Stories* (now on Netflix), is a writer on an upcoming 20th Century/Disney+ live action fantasy series, and is developing an original fantasy pilot as part of the 2022 Ojala Ignition Fellowship. Her work has been supported by fellowships and grants from Oregon Literary Arts, Vermont Studio Center, Film Independent, Regional Arts and Culture Council, and Oregon Arts Commission. Stephanie is also a Tarot reader and instructor of poetry and divination. She is making headway on a Major Arcana tarot deck inspired by occult animism. Find out more: obsurobeach.com / Instagram: @Tarot_Obscuro.

Erik L. Arneson is a practicing magician who got his first Tarot deck in the late 1980s and has been working with the cards in some capacity ever since. His writing has appeared in a number of periodicals and in both volumes of *A Small Collection of Specialized Spreads*. With decades of experience in Western esotericism, he has lectured at several conferences and taught classes on ceremonial magic, Tarot, and the Art of Memory. Erik is the host of the Arnemancy Podcast and writes about Tarot, magic, and the occult on his site arnemancy.com and @arnemancy on Instagram.

Roberta Aylward creative practice is driven by curiosity and experimentation. With a focus on process and materials, her abstract work documents unseen memories, feelings and emotional landscapes. She received her BFA from The College of Santa Fe in 1991. Her work has been included in exhibitions at the Tacoma Art Museum, Oregon College of Art and Craft, Marghitta Feldman Gallery, The Gretchen Schuette Art Gallery, and Umpqua Valley Arts Association. She practices art-making daily in her Pacific Northwest studio, creating paintings, drawings, sculpture and collage. Find her online at robertaaylward.com and on IG at @robertaaylward.

A diviner since the summer of 1990, **Amanda Bell** finds that she reads tarot the way she does most things— she pays attention, She listens and she stays feral. She is a helper, a finder, and a maker of things-become-real. She can be found creating spaces + events for readers + collectors, helping creators make the divination tool of their dreams, and talking about cards on indiedeckreview.com.

Charlie Claire Burgess (they/them) is a tarot practitioner, author, illustrator, and deck creator whose work centers on queering the tarot for a radically liberated life. They believe tarot is a powerful tool for personal revolution that can help create better individual and collective futures, which is the subject of their first book, *Radical Tarot* (Hay House, 2023). Their tarot deck, Fifth Spirit Tarot, was crowdfunded and self-published in 2020 and will be released in a new, mass market edition from Hay House in early 2023. Charlie is currently working on two more decks, occasionally recording new episodes of their podcast The Word Witch, and sometimes teaching tarot classes online and in so-called Portland, Oregon, where they live with their spouse and an extreme number of houseplants and fantasy novels. Find their work at thewordwitchtarot.com and follow along @the.word.witch on Instagram.

Jennifer Ciraulo is a tarot reader and licensed therapist living in New York City. She received her graduate degree in social work from the University of Illinois at Chicago, and is certified in tarot reading by 22 Teachings School of Hermetic Science and Magical Arts. In her work as a reader and therapist, her mission is to assist in her client's healing and alignment with their most authentic and empowered version of themselves. As a proud member of the recovery community, she is passionate about harm reduction and ending the stigma around mental health and substance use disorders. Her hobbies include running, spending time with her husband and cats, laughing at memes, and watching reality television. She can be found at sacredspacesnyc.com; sacredspacestarot.com; and on Instagram @jeniferjupiter1111.

105

Corey Coppola first learned the tarot around the age of six from his parents and continued to study the cards into adulthood. After reading professionally for eleven years, he now reads only for friends and family and is focused on sharing his knowledge to help people connect better with themselves and others. He lives in Portland, OR. Connect with him for a reading/ritual on Instagram: @metaphysic_advisory_counsel.

Juanita Esperanto has been reading Tarot cards for many lifetimes. Self-taught and a natural intuitive, she's worked in Portland, San Francisco, and for a 1-800 psychic hotline. Connect with her online at juanitaesperanto.com and on Instagram: @juanitaesperanto.

Denise Harwood is a student of the Tarot.

Skylar Haven (they/them) is a space holder. They support others in their healing, connection with their body and with finding deeper ease and personal power in life. They are queer, trans non-binary, poly, and work as a sex coach, bodyworker, and yoga therapist with a focus on topics related to sex, embodiment, health issues and wellness. Skylar's relationship with tarot is always evolving, and they often work with tarot as a way of connecting with intuitive knowing, reflection, and healing. In 2021 Skylar and their partner Trish founded Indie Tarot, a tarot shop focused on supporting and selling independently produced tarot and oracle decks created by LGBTQIA+ and BIPOC artists. You can find more about them and their work at: queersomatics.co, collaborativemotion.com, indie-tarot.co, and on Instagram: @indie.tarot.

Via Hedera is a California-born, Pacific Northwest-based sculptor, folklore enthusiast, writer and occult practitioner operating a blog dedicated to folkloric witchcraft in the Americas, modern animism and sacred art. Growing up in a multicultural and spiritually diverse community, she dedicates her time to the study of traditional witchcraft practices, ancestor veneration, and all things magical. Her book *Folkloric Witchcraft and the Multicultural Experience: A Crucible at the Crossroads* is one witch's love letter to the presence of animism and magic in the Americas and details not only her personal relationship to folkmagic, but her love of shared magical experiences between diverse peoples. Find her on IG as @viahedera and online at viahedera.com.

Hannah Kim is a tarot reader and musician currently based in Seoul, South Korea. Reach out to her on Instagram for sliding scale readings: @hags_1111. Her music can be found on SoundCloud under "hags": https://soundcloud.com/hags1111.

Natalie Kirby is a full-blown Gemini who loves the magic elixir called coffee. She's in the midst of a magical journey—don't stop believing." Find her online at atarotstoryteller@gmail.com and on Instagram as @atarotstoryteller.

Sonya Miranda (They/Them) is a tarot fan, just like you. They've been using tarot as a visual and artistic tool to help them through their journey of recovery from codependency. Almost from the beginning they realized they needed tailored spreads for this particular work. Over the past few years they've created a few spreads and shared them on IG. Mostly, Sonya reads for themself and uses others' spreads when they seem to fit with what is needed at the time. Sonya also enjoys learning about the political side of tarot, queering it, and breaking out of the gender binary with it. If you'd like to follow Sonya's personal tarot journal and occasionally catch their spreads follow on IG: @whitcheewalrus. For their art and hobbies (and fur babies): @whimsywalrus.

Joseph O'Sullivan is a writer, journalist, and creator. He lives in Olympia, Wash. Follow his adventures on IG @speedthepilgrim.

Alan Pérez believes that cartomancy is a language we can use as a way of understanding ourselves as part of the Universe and as a form of prayer. (¿How is it that I fit in the World around me? ¿How do I feel about that? ¿How can I ask the Universe for guidance?) Recently he's been interested in how cartomancy, like accents, can add nuance and understanding to our conversations. Using different techniques in readings is like understanding how grammar and sentence structure across languages allow for both greater understanding and ambiguity. Some ideas do not always translate, but cartomancy allows us to continue to be active participants within and without as we ask and listen for guidance. As we learn to understand context and nuance we begin to see words and phrases form from our readings, and with honest translation we can communicate with the Universe. Still, the responsibility of translating accurately, for oneself and especially when reading for others, is vital to conversing honestly with the Universe. (¿Whose voices are we not hearing?) If you want to chat or check out some fun art you can find him on Instagram as @vulpes_veloz or email him brm2pdx@gmail.com.

Janaki Phillips is currently a PhD candidate in anthropology at the University of Michigan. Her dissertation research is a comparative study of tarot reading practices in Los Angeles, California and Mumbai, India. She is interested in the different cultural norms around tarot: how tarot is used as a divinatory tool, the intersection of tarot and social media, the recent rise in its popularity, how people are using tarot to deal with uncertainty, as well as different cultural orientations towards the future. In addition to being a scholar of contemporary tarot, she has also been a long time practitioner. You can find her offering daily draws with help from her feline accomplice Madame Bathsheba on Instagram @cat.o.mancy.

Cherri Roden is a student of Tarot who believes the highest calling of the cards is to assist us in introspection and exploration. Her spreads invite us to dig deeper and go farther to gain insights that help us evolve.

Jess Rollar lives in the Arizona White Mountains and is the card reader and artist behind Coffee with the Fool. She's the creator and illustrator of the Squid Cake Marseille and Strange Lenormand decks. Learn more at coffeewiththefool.com and on IG: @coffeewiththefool.

Selah Saterstrom practices a Southern-family style of card reading and divination. With Kristen E. Nelson, she curates Four Queens, a platform for Divinatory Poetics. She is the author of five books, including The Pink Institution, Slab, Rancher and Ideal Sugesstions: Essays in Divinatory Poetics. She lives with her wife and daughter in Colorado. Find out more at @fourqueensdivination on Instagram.

Ann Seletos is a tarot reader and reiki practitioner in Los Angeles, CA, hailing from Phoenix, AZ. She owns and operates Sundown Tarot, named for the liminal space and transformational state of the sunset, embracing the mysteries of the desert. She is currently a resident tarot reader at The Mystic Museum in Burbank and reads for private clients all over the world. You can also find her drumming in bands and DJing 45rpm records around the LA area. She is a lover of literature and writing, and enjoys creating tarot spread for each new and full moon of the year. You can book with Ann on her website sundowntarot.com and find her on Instagram at @sundowntarot and @ann__eliza.

Sir Bran the Blessed (they/them) is a hereditary enchantress, witch, and conjurer who grew up practicing old school Hoodoo, New Orleans Voodoo, European Witchcraft, and Curanderismo. Many students and clients throughout the Portland community come to them for readings, magickal education, and various tricks, spells, and fixes. Bran believes that one should know the rules and then transcend them through rigorous study, humor, practice, and innovation, an approach they apply to their personal practice. They are currently writing a series of zines and an occult book titled *Mixed Kid Magick: Journeys in Magick through Racial and Queer Identity and Intersectionality*. In addition, Bran is a founder and leader of the PDX innovative community coven Zephyrhaus. They love pizza rolls and at some point intend to get married on a unicorn. (And yes, they will wear white. Ok, cream). Instagram: @sirbrantheblessed; Twitter: @sirbrantheblesd.

Leah Sottile is a Portland-based journalist, essayist and short fiction writer. She is the author of the book *When the Moon Turns to Blood* (June 2022). Her work has been published in The *New York Times Magazine*, *The Washington Post*, *Rolling Stone* and other magazines. Her fiction has most recently been published in *Evergreen: Grim Tales & Verses from the Gloomy Northwest*. She uses divination decks as creative prompts and is at work designing her first oracle system. Subscribe to her newsletter "The Truth Does Not Change According to Your Ability to Stomach It!" at leahsottile.substack.com. Find her @leah_sottile on Twitter.

Lars Sparby is a trollmann and magic(k) worker who practices highly localized heksekunst in the old town of Oslo, Norway. Twenty years ago he borrowed a tarot deck from a friend, and things were never the same again. Synchronically this is about the same time he was granted the gift of invisibility. The rest, as they say, is destiny. He can usually be found wandering around in cemeteries but also unusually online at trolldomsvart.com and unitedmindarts.com as well as @trolldomsvart and @unitedmindarts on Instagram.

Coleman Stevenson is the author of three poetry collections (*Light Sleeper*, *Breakfast*, and *The Accidental Rarefication of Pattern #5609*), several books about the Tarot including *The Dark Exact Tarot Guide*, and a book of essays on creativity accompanying the card game *Metaphysik*. Her writing has appeared in many literary journals and anthologies and on the website tarot.com. In addition to her work as a designer of tarot and oracle decks through her company The Dark Exact, her fine art work, exhibited in galleries around the Pacific Northwest, focuses on the intersections between image and text. She has been a guest curator for various gallery spaces in the Portland, Oregon, area, and has taught tarot, poetry, design theory, and cultural studies at a number of different institutions there, most currently for the Literary Arts Delve series, which includes seminars at the Portland Art Museum. Find her work at online at colemanstevenson.com and @darkexact on Instagram.

Zoë Torres is an adept tarot reader, Reiki master, teacher of Reiki classes, ritualist, and trauma informed massage therapist. A gatherer of all that is fleeting, her love affair with life, and experiencing the five senses as well as what lies beyond them, stokes her curiosity for the arcane and obscure. You can find her on Instagram @readingsbyzoe or on readingsbyzoe.com.

Greg Traw is an esoteric artist, musician, and creator of the Dracxiodos Tarot. He considers all creative practice a channeling and an interplay between spirit, sense experience, materials, space and time. He is the bassist for the heavy progressive rock group Kvasir, loves the outdoors and lives in Portland, Oregon. Learn more about his work at nohheechul.com and @nohheechul / @dracxiodostarot on Instagram.

Melanie Trowbridge has worked with the Tarot for over 30 years and has recently begun to deepen her insight and relationship with each card through acceptance and compassion of all of life's circumstances. Her philosophy in any divination work is that one must not be biased or fearful of what will be revealed but instead remain open to receiving the most information and benefit from tools of higher insight. She believes that we must face divination work with courage to make more guided actions in the light of truth and progress in our individual paths. Justice is found only where balance and truth are achieved.

Liz Worth is a tarot reader and writer. She can be reached at lizworth.com.

ACKNOWLEDGEMENTS

My gratitude to the students in Spread Design Basics. Erik and I were honored to work with you!

Thank you to Alexa Gaynor for your proofing assistance.

A huge thanks to my friend Camas who let me spend two productive weeks in her guest room while I focused on finishing this project without the usual daily interruptions. This book's completion was fueled by California sunrises.

NOTES

NOTES

NOTES